"When we first started looking into our family members' tempera-ments, we had no idea how valuable the information we gained would be. The most significant help initially came in realizing that, as we jok-ingly came to refer to it, we are a family of three 'peas' and one 'pod.' The 'pod' is our daughter. It seemed we were always somehow out of sync with her. Learning to understand her temperament and how it differed from her father's, brother's, and mine gave us insights that made our job as parents much easier."

— *Linda Goshorn*
mother of elementary-aged children

"As a new stepmother of a 9-year-old, the Myers-Briggs Indicator gave me wonderful insight into understanding her preferences. It made our family adjustment so much easier and more focused on God's design rather than on our preconceived expectations."

—*Kay Baldwin*
stepmother

"Understanding temperament has helped me be a more effective mid-dle school music teacher. Not only does it help me recognize my own strengths and weaknesses, but it helps me accept and deal with a wide array of students. It has helped me be more patient with those students who are different from me, and it has explained why some students are easier for me to deal with."

—*Kathy McDonald*
middle school music teacher

"Temperament understanding released us to appreciate our oldest son, whom we all considered a bit weird. Because Ryan is so different from his siblings and from either of us, the entire family was constantly at odds. How relieved we were to discover that Ryan's personality type falls into a unique 1% with those who need a great deal of peace and privacy to work on intense intellectual pursuits. After receiving this information, we gave him a room away from family noise. We began to celebrate who he was and stopped nagging him about dating or being involved in team sports."

Lois and Ron Short

"The Myers-Briggs Indicator has made the biggest impact on my life. I was always the square peg in the round hole—never quite fitting in. Now I've learned that each part of my personality is a gift from God. Instead of looking at the negatives of each trait, I focus on the positives. Now I am more confident in accepting my inborn limitations. My two sons who are complete opposites know that I love and accept them for who they are."

—Mary Ann Albright
mother of young children

"When my family attended the family enrichment seminar led by Jim and Ruth Ward, I discovered that all my family members were very spontaneous while I am rigidly structured. After attempting to structure everyone for 21 years, with much frustration, I have begun to accept each member more as they are. It is much more peaceful in our home learning to work together instead of expecting them to think and act like me."

—Larry Theisen
father of teens

"Temperament information is an invaluable tool I use everyday in relationships with others. No relationship has challenged and stretched me more than that with our first child. Jordan was about 3 years old when I realized I had to manage him differently than I needed to be managed as a child. My day began with a list of ideas and plans I would present to him. He would fight me and upset the plans—even fun activities! Your seminar taught me that he likes surprises, not plans. We are both happier if he isn't burdened with my desired schedule and we allow the day to unfold as a surprise to him.

"Jordan never wanted to be treated like a child, so we dealt with him as an adult in listening and considering his well thought-out ideas. He is often a few steps ahead of me in his logical approach to things. I have learned to give him the quiet and alone time he needs as an introvert, which is different from me. I like to be around people constantly and to be involved in lots of activity. Jordan and his dad are 'wired' the same way. I get better results with Jordan if I mimic Mike's approach with him."

—Jan Ziegenbein
mother of a young child

COACHING KIDS

PRACTICAL TIPS FOR EFFECTIVE COMMUNICATION

JIM AND RUTH WARD

SMYTH&HELWYS
PUBLISHING, INCORPORATED · MACON, GEORGIA

Smyth & Helwys Publishing, Inc.
6316 Peake Road
Macon, Georgia 31210-3960
1-800-747-3016
©1999 by Smyth & Helwys Publishing
All rights reserved.
Printed in the United States of America.

Jim and Ruth Ward

The paper used in this publication meets the minimum
requirements of American National Standard for Information
Sciences—Permanence of Paper for Printed Library Materials.
ANSI Z39.48–1984. (alk. paper)

Library of Congress Cataloging-in-Publication Data

Ward, Ruth McRoberts.
    Coaching Kids: Practical Tips for Effective Communication
    pp.   cm.
    Includes bibliographical references.
    1. Parent and child. 2. Interpersonal communication.
    3. Interpersonal relations. I. Ward, Jim. II. Title.
    HV769.W37   1999
    649'.1—dc21   98-30885
                                                         CIP
ISBN1-57312-250-5

Contents

Foreword

Helping children to mature leaves even the best of parents feeling frenzied, frazzled, and fed up. There is no way around it: these are the years that cause those of us who must parent to doubt our capability, sanity, and emotional strength.

My wife and I have at long last reached those golden promises of Proverbs 22:6—"Train children in the right way, and when old, they will not stray." We tried through the seasons of tempest and Tylenol to follow the wisdom writer. Finally, our dreams have come true. Our children are now "clothed and in their right minds." Indeed, they are living beautiful lives, and we have a grandson who, in a few years, will be entering his teenage years. . . . I may live long enough to see my children playing the games of parenting a teenager. What shall I do? Smile with an odd sense of recompense that they are, at last, eating what they once dished up? I think not. I think we shall celebrate their passage as a season that makes life wise.

Jim and Ruth Ward have written very practically of tension years of our lives. Thanks to them for walking the path before us and publishing this little road map. They can serve as the guardians and counselors who bring us all together in a new era of family togetherness. Let this book become your guide in cross-generational survival—nay, our cross-generational friendship. It may become a handbook for those who have yet to make the teen trek through the stress-filled years of pain and celebration.

Be faithful to the Ward kind of parenting, and you and your children may finally arrive at the image of Christ, and you may discover that you like your kids after all because of something as warm, weird, and wonderful as faith.

—Calvin Miller

In Appreciation of

- Parents, teachers, and caregivers in our seminars and classes, along with clients, who have shared their experiences and struggles for new attitudes, concepts, and language

- Our family and friends who encouraged us to give them a simple guide for effective parenting

- Scott Painter, our good friend and computer guru who rescued us many times at strange hours during the preparation of the manuscript

- The staff at Smyth & Helwys, especially our warm and patient editor, Jackie Riley, whose expert editing sharpened our focus and makes this book more readable

Dedicated to our children
Kay, David, Julia Beth, Roger
and their wonderful children

Introduction

Did you solemnly swear when you were younger that "my kids are not going to talk back, act like brats, and fight like I did when I was a kid"? Did you also mutter criticisms about unruly kids: "Why don't those parents control their kids and make them behave?" We thought parenting would be a snap because we loved each other, had a balanced view of life, wanted a family, and were committed to our task. But we soon discovered that parenting requires more than that. We needed some coaching.

Are you in the stages of making this discovery? Do you regard your children as empty vessels with your responsibility being to stuff them with information and rules on how they should think, feel, and function? Perhaps your parents tried, like their peers, to create clones of themselves, repeating what was said and done to them. If so, you have lots of company. By following these approaches, many parents unwittingly set themselves up for anger, disappointment, and frustration if and when their children resist, rebel, or fail. We have discovered, however, that rather than empty vessels requiring filling from without, children more closely resemble flower bulbs that are intricately pre-programmed for splendid blooming.

"Tender bulbs" need to be handled gently, placed in suitable soil, exposed to proper light, given adequate water, supplied with specific soil nutrients, and protected from disease, harsh weather, and encroachment from other plants. Until bulbs are provided the atmosphere and nutrients to grow and bloom, one can barely imagine what beautiful creations can occur. We can expect our children to respond with unique vitality to the same deliberate groundwork and careful stimuli. Our 4 children have bloomed, and now we are enjoying the blossoming of our 12 grandchildren.

The majority of adults with whom we dialogue in classes, seminars, and counseling sessions lament: "My parents never understood me." "I was emotionally undermined and abused." Many complain that they received a steady diet of negative or scant parental dialogue. A 58-year-old man shared,

> When I was 10 years old, my father assigned me a repair job he thought I was either smart enough or old enough to do. When I botched the job, he squinted his eyes and said, "I'm so ashamed of you that I'm not even going to tell my friends you're my son." His words haunt me to this day, especially when I'm down.

He wept. Imagine, a 5-second statement inflicting 48 years of emotional pain! You, too, may be carrying around a childhood put-down.

Problems can arise when your children prefer to relate to society in a different fashion than you relate. They may pick up information differently, and perhaps possess temperament preferences that go against your grain. You may be very reserved and quiet-spoken but have an all-smiles, loquacious, never still, outgoing child—a startling and distressing phenomenon for both of you.

Are you like your parents? Do you think your kids want to be just like you? A 40-year-old mother of teens said recently, "It's hard to be who I really am when I've gotten so used to being who my parents wanted me to be." Many adults express the desire to be as unlike their parents as possible. Consequently, for the sake of our children's mental and emotional health, we must learn to allow them to think, feel, and function differently rather than try to force them to become someone God did not design them to be. Granted, this is not an easy assignment, but it is a reachable goal.

The majority of current parenting material rightly deals with educating offspring to avoid inappropriate conduct, understand spiritual concepts, accept responsibility, and build confidence to become financially independent, self-disciplined, and socially successful. But when this teaching is laced with an empty-vessel attitude overlooking natural preferences, children are manipulated into ill-fitting molds, attitudes, and opinions, which can leave them feeling insecure, unfulfilled, and disillusioned.

In *Coaching Kids: Practical Tips for Effective Communication* we offer practical tips for positive and diplomatic dialogue achieved by respecting individual temperaments. We examine the integral, crucial influence of how you were reared and how the childhood of each of your parents contribute to the delicate but difficult privilege and task of parenting. To equip you to appreciate and understand your own uniqueness and that of your children, we include an interpretation of personality preferences mixed with practical application of the principles.

Experience has convinced us that mixing courteous dialogue with temperament understanding is the healthiest, surest, and most pleasant way for kids to develop inner self-discipline and be prepared for successful adulthood and parenthood. We are especially delighted at how understanding temperament impacts and removes the sting of sibling rivalry.

"But you don't understand my situation," you say. "I'm a single parent." Or, "I'm trying to live in a blended family with someone else's children." Or, "You have no idea how awful it is trying to parent with my impossible ex." We are aware that many of you face complex challenges in relating to a former spouse, your current spouse, stepchildren, and/or children from a new relationship. We are also astounded to learn that today 5 to 7 million children are being reared by their grandparents. The number is predicted to rise to 14 million by the year 2000. We admire the selflessness of anyone parenting a second time around—a tough assignment. Perhaps you are one of them. So, grandparents, we know you are out there looking for immediate relief. We think this book can help you, too. In fact, it will be of value to anyone who works with children either now or in the future—future parents, babysitters, daycare workers, public and private school teachers, homeschoolers, and church teachers/ leaders.

Effective communication with kids of all ages and situations requires time, patience, listening, talking, respect, understanding, appreciation, much prayer, and in some cases support groups. In our opinion, respect—for self and child—tops the list as the best guarantee for successful parenting. Our goal is to provide the most practical helps possible to assist you as you coach your children. Think of this book as a resource to encourage you over the hurdles of changes and growth they will experience.

—Ruth and Jim Ward

*Names and situations have been changed for the sake of confidentiality.

TIP #1

Break the cycle of passed-on parenting.

Pretend you are a child again—impressionable, tender, free, excited, curious, teachable, accepting, vulnerable, honest. Just slip your shoes off and wiggle your toes to help you relax and reminisce. Describe in one word your childhood. Consider these questions:

- How was your childhood affected by your siblings, education, extracurricular activities, living situation, and parents' income?
- Do you recall being ignored, misunderstood, or receiving the silent treatment?
- Were your parents yellers, screamers, or commanders?
- Did you receive unreasonable spankings, angry beatings, or verbal put-downs?

Now, think back to the following ages in your life:

5 or 6
- Did a parent or guardian make you feel individually important?
- Can you recall something significant that was said to you or about you?
- Were your emotional and physical hurts acknowledged and tended to fairly and tenderly?
- Did significant adults in your life keep their promises?
- How were you disciplined, or were you just punished for what you did?

9 or 10
- Were you permitted to play games or participate in activities that interested you?
- How did your main adult caregiver regard you?
- Were your ideas or suggestions sought and/or respected?
- Were you affirmed or encouraged in your studies, hobbies, and recreational and sports activities?
- Did any adult seem interested in your world?
- Did you receive approval for trying, or only criticism and disapproval when you made mistakes?
- Were you corrected rather than directed?

12 or 13
- Were your dreams about your future respected, or did you keep them private for fear of criticism?
- Do you remember being compared to a sibling, cousin, or friend in looks, size, abilities, or disposition?
- Did you consider yourself different, inadequate, unlovable, or even a bit weird?
- What were your parents' opinions of you?
- Did anyone attempt to inspire you toward future achievements?
- Did you regard yourself as an important team member, or more as a disruption to an adult's schedule?
- Were your physical needs accepted as legitimate, or were they grudgingly filled?
- What method of guidance did your parents use with you?

Late Teens–Early 20s
- How did you relate to your father? mother? siblings? grandparents? teachers?
- Did you feel joy about life?
- Can you recall any particular statement made to you, name you were called, or opinion stated about you that has remained in the recesses of your heart and mind?

• Did your parents' eyes light up when they saw you?
• Did you feel important? respected? intelligent? satisfied with
  how you were developing?
• Did you like yourself?
• Were you encouraged to share your dreams and feelings?

When we ask seminar attendees and counselees to describe in one word their childhood, the majority choose words such as horrendous, empty, hateful, controlled, unhappy, uncontrolled, miserable, awful, lonely, demoralizing, unkind, abusive, unfair, or boring. Many of us would offer a similar evaluation.

If you were treated inappropriately as a child, you have probably dealt with guilt, fear, shame, low self-esteem, and/or loss of self-respect. If you were subjected to one-sided lectures and arbitrary punishment, you know full well that such methods did not produce a feeling of well-being—perhaps obedience, but more often disillusionment and anger. Yet, despite the inadequate parenting we might have received, whether we intend to or not, we tend to repeat the pattern.

The Perils of Passed-On Parenting

It's like I'm obsessed. Since I wasn't talked to rationally as a child, only hit and yelled at, that seems to be the first method I choose when I'm stressed. It's frightening.

I catch myself impulsively yelling, hitting, berating, ignoring, and generally being disrespectful of my child even though I know it's wrong. I vowed I wouldn't engage in it because I hated that treatment when I was young.

I was never allowed to touch the television until I was 10. It doesn't make sense that a 5-year-old should have a privilege I never had.

Whether you intend to or not, your parenting skills may resemble those of your parents. Likewise, they probably parented you like they were parented, passing on both superior and inferior skills, attitudes, and techniques they learned by the OJT method ("On-the-Job Training"). In many cases your parents were wise, positive, and respectful, and their homes were secure and healthy safety nets. The scary part, however, is that your grandparents and parents were just as prone to repeat harmful cycles as good ones, even though they disliked and disagreed with the methods of punishment rendered on them. If they are honest with themselves, they may still grieve over the residue of scarred relationships and damaged self-esteem stemming from being misunderstood and mistreated.

A counselee, seeking to overcome the effects of a lifetime of poor parenting, recounted how her mother repeatedly told her she was "an accident." In the words of her mother, "I already had my son and daughter, and then you were born." As a child, the woman was mistreated and abused mentally, physically, and sexually. Consequently, she developed low self-esteem and was involved in several abusive marriages.

A 35-year-old woman remembered watching the television show "Leave It to Beaver" when she was a child and thinking what a strange family that was—nothing like hers. Then, it dawned on her that it was *her* family that was not normal. She had an alcoholic mother and a raging father. She had gotten used to inferior parenting.

Many people fail to recognize their own rearing as defective. Many of our parents assume that how they were talked to and treated must have been right. Have you heard your parents make any of the following statements?

• *"Dad believed in using the razor strap, but I lived through it."*
• *"We knew if we got paddled at school, we'd get another one when we got home; but I turned out okay."*

• *"All of us kids were terrified of Dad."*
• *"My parents meant well and did a good job considering their limitations and the times."*

How is it with you? Have you caught yourself yelling for control and resorting to screaming? Have you discovered how slapping grows into spanking, and spanking into beatings and fights? Often, the more a procedure or attitude is repeated, the worse it becomes.

Does Practice Make Perfect?

"We did the best job we could," our parents and grandparents usually defend. "We were hardly more than children ourselves," they often add. While becoming a parent is natural and relatively easy, preparing a child to love properly, live responsibly, and eventually leave the nest is the most demanding and unprescribed assignment we can assume, and is performed for the most part by novices.

In parenting, practice does not always make perfect. In many instances, practice just reinforces bad habits instilled from the past. Unlike tinkering on a car or fiddling with a computer, experimenting on children often generates perpetual repercussions. Fortunately, children are resilient and can adjust to many honest, *occasional* blunders. However, when mistakes become the norm and evolve into physical, emotional, or verbal abuse, not only will children probably require professional help at some time, but detrimental parenting cycles may be repeated for generations until broken by an enlightened grown-up.

Some folks think that if you provide for your children's physical needs, make them work, teach them to be honest and obedient, and expose them to the church or synagogue, then you are a pretty decent parent. They believe "the best thing is to boot kids out of the nest after high school and let them sink or swim."

But this is not always the best approach. Consider the words of Scott Peck:

> Parents must ask not so much, "What do I want from my child?" as "What, from the broader viewpoint of an ideal observer, does this God-given child most need that we can offer?"[1]

Competent parenting does not happen automatically or easily; it involves more than merely taking physical care of children and responding to current problems. You are always the parent of your children no matter how old they are, and most of us will unconsciously maintain a measure of responsibility for them. We have observed retired parents anguishing over their 40-plus offspring's failure to achieve, adjust socially, or succeed maritally. "Where did we go wrong?" they ask themselves. We can't take all the blame for how our children turn out—or all the credit, for that matter.

Competent parenting requires wisdom, good modeling, selflessness, education, unconditional love, open-mindedness, consistency, understanding the various temperaments, and honest communication.

Breaking the Cycle

Avoiding or correcting parenting mistakes of the past requires education, humility, discipline, energy, and in many cases understanding and forgiveness for parents who themselves received little parenting education or encouragement. To break these terrible cycles, remind yourself, "What was reality for me doesn't have to be inevitable for my child."

Take a candid look at your childhood to identify healthy methods and attitudes and also unwise, outdated, and inappropriate parenting attitudes and techniques that were applied to you. Strive to incorporate positive parenting such as affirming your children daily. Verbally express your love for them. Acknowledge approved behaviors, for example, "I notice that you put your books away," or, "I like being with you."

Do not pass on what you did not like. Decide which cycles are worthy of repetition and which ones are injurious and should be discontinued. Set in motion positive, workable, and constructive cycles. Get ready for potential disapproval, however.

Grandparents are often disgusted, verbally critical, and threatened when their children adopt different parenting styles for their grandchildren. They complain,

> Our grandchildren expect to be treated as equals—grownups. Why, when our kids were little, they never questioned what we said or did. We never allowed them to. . . . Our grandkids don't respect possessions. They have too much.

Respectfully discussing with your parents the pros and cons of parenting styles of yesterday and today will relieve some of their anguish and fears and make your job easier.

We do not propose that any of you confront aging parents regarding honest mistakes that were common practice in an era 40 or 50 years ago. That action would be counterproductive. However, one of the most revealing and helpful personal exercises is to research a little deeper to discover how your parents were parented and how your grandparents were parented. You will be delightfully surprised how that insight will release anger and bitterness and ultimately lead to forgiveness for mistakes, neglect, and abuse. After completing such an assignment, one lady said,

> How can I hold a grudge against my mother knowing what she put up with as a child and what her parents went through? Truly an eye-opener!

Conclusion

We have never met anyone who experienced a flawless childhood or anyone who did not have to work through some type of child-hood crisis. Even the most conscientious and knowledgeable parents make honest mistakes, but we are confident that you are striving to avoid as many parental pitfalls as possible. The best you can do is to be open for instruction and willing to learn from the mistakes of others.

Parenting courses or support groups are a relatively new phe-nomenon your parents probably did not have. Many of our parents just instinctively chose to avoid negative styles they expe-rienced and managed to substitute positive, respectful ways. We marvel at the wisdom of our parents and count our blessings.

Just as many of us have been enlightened by Dale Carnegie's course *How to Win Friends and Influence People*, we are wise to cultivate that same type of diplomatic dialogue with our chil-dren and teens in order to influence them effectively. Our goal is to benefit all youth by coaching you to break inferior parenting patterns and conversational cycles by respecting each child's individual temperament and incorporating a positive style and attitude that will also make parenting more fulfilling.

We compare our approach to that of an unskilled person picking out a tune on the piano, making many mistakes but improving with practice; to a trained musician playing with both hands, skillfully reading notes and dynamics from a musical score, but still making a few mistakes but not as serious. We have watched our approach work for many parents and grandparents, and we are delighted to share our good news with you.

TIP #2
Communicate with respect.

Do you recall being praised by someone for something you did? Do you recall a specific statement someone said in the past about how nice or thoughtful you were? You can probably still remember how good you felt about yourself. Contrast that feeling with the times you have felt an inch high or like crawling into a hole when someone embarrassed you or attacked you about how you looked, talked, or performed.

Through respectful dialogue we communicate affirmation and individual acceptance, encourage self-discipline, and validate a person's worth. Through faulty dialogue we deflate someone's motivation to try and injure a person's self-image. Before children learn to speak, they pick up through conversation, body language, and tone whether or not they are valued and respected. Good conversational skills cultivate constructive communication.

Conversation is the art of transferring ideas and implanting values. The dynamics of dialogue hinge around listening creatively, knowing when and how to speak, and learning to edit speech. Therefore, our intention in this section is to identify faulty dialogue and the magnitude of emotional damage incurred because of it. This chapter focuses on the intrinsic influence of negative speech.

Destructive Dialogue

Many of us unwittingly engage in inappropriate and unhealthy conversational habits copied from our parents, the marketplace, the media, television, books, movies, and other sources. Conscientious young parents with whom we counsel are dismayed to discover their thoughtless, habitual involvement in destructive and hurtful family dialogue. "We just fell into a nasty, lazy pattern," one dad confessed.

Verbal abuse seems to have increased as physical abuse laws have become more rigidly enforced. Many counselors claim verbal abuse to be even more harmful than physical abuse, causing mental abuse that deeply affects one's self-esteem. One instance of abuse usually spawns other violations.

The following offensive tactics are by no means exhaustive, but they cover the most common infractions. As you read these descriptions, check how many of these abuses you suffered as a child and unconsciously pass on to your children.

Searing Sarcasm

- *How many times must I repeat the same thing? Are you deaf? Then why don't you listen?*
- *You are so rude. Were you brought up in a jungle? That's where you belong, you know.*
- *What's the matter with you, anyhow? Are you crazy or just stupid? I know where you'll end up!*

Sarcasm is a humorous statement or remark with a cruel hook made with the intention of embarrassing or injuring the self-respect of someone, usually by drawing attention to a weakness or failure of that person. It is inverted teasing—hurtful comments meant to be funny.

According to Haim Ginott, who wrote the above quotes, a parent with a gift for sarcasm is a serious mental health hazard. "A wizard with words, he erects his own sound barrier to effective communication. . . . Such a parent may not even be aware that his remarks are attacks that invite counterattacks, that his comments block communication by stirring children to preoccupation with revenge fantasies."[2]

Sarcasm is difficult to eliminate. There is something witty and clever about hurling our opinion or judgment all rolled up in unique observations or possibilities about a person. It makes others laugh and still gets our point across. Eliminating sarcasm is almost as hard as giving up chocolate—or peanut butter, if that's your passion. But our world would be a much happier place without hurtful sarcasm.

Negative Name-Calling

• *Cool it, Motor Mouth.*
• *Time to get up, Dumb Dumb.*
• *Make way for Willie Wide Load.*
• *Brace yourself for Amazon Woman!*
• *How's my little Buzzard Boy doing today?*

What was your nickname as a kid? Did you like it? Do you remember who named you? What other names were you called? "It's part of growing up," some parents defend. "We all put up with it. Kids have to learn to be tough and to ignore names."

The old adage "Sticks and stones may break my bones, but words will never harm me," is far from the truth. Names hurt. For instance, "Bucktooth Beaver," "Fatso," "Piano Legs," "Four Eyes," "Shorty," and "Skinny" all call attention to a physical difference. Names often stick. Children are likely to become what they are called, for example: "Slowpoke," "Showoff," "Lazy," "Pig," "Whale," and "Spoiled Brat."

"I was called selfish and stupid so often," Grace shared, "that I honestly believed I was until I went away to college. My C's and D's turned to A's and B's, and I made the Dean's honor roll and graduated in the top 10% of my class."

Haim Ginott taught us to attack the event and not the character of the person. Specifically, you may say something Charlie *did* was stupid, but do not call *him* stupid. Similarly, do not call a child an angel or wonderful. Rather, assign appreciation to what the child did. Instead of saying, "You're wonderful for cleaning out the garage," say, "The garage has never looked so clean."

Nasty and foul names too offensive to print and often preceded by profanity and vulgar talk by parents, siblings, relatives, and friends especially leave deep emotional marks. All forms of crude name-calling, including wounding racial slurs, must be strictly avoided because children think about and repeat what they hear. In addition, recovering from the feelings of inferiority resulting from being called names often develops into a major adult struggle.

Painful Put-Downs

• *Pretty is as pretty does.*
• *You have the brains of a bird.*
• *You'll never amount to anything.*
• *You're like a catfish—all mouth and no brains.*
• *Why can't you be smart/neat/well-behaved . . . like Harold?*
• *You must have been behind the door when brains were given out.*
• *That's not painting; it's painting by numbers. Anyone can do that!*

Put-downs are acts or statements that embarrass or denigrate another. They are close relatives of sarcasm. They emphasize a person's mental or physical inabilities or inadequacies. There seems to be no particular motive to spewing put-downs, but they rather emerge out of a snide, surface, general, abrupt reaction. Shame is closely related to put-downs aimed at disapproval of the total person.

When children who are trying to improve or overcome a personal obstacle or family problem hear only about their failures, put-downs can significantly impede their progress and feelings of self-worth. Comparing a child to a sibling or peer often boomerangs into lifelong bitter resentment.

It is especially difficult today to teach children to avoid parroting put-downs. Movies, family television programs, cartoons, video games, and the internet are infested with them. Children ingesting this type of discourse day after day face a tremendous struggle not to repeat it. What goes in eventually comes out. We face a tremendous challenge in cleaning up ugly talk.

Ripping Ridicule

• *So, are you going to drive with one hand on the wheel and one thumb in your mouth?*
• *If we could take your head and put it on your friend's body, we'd have a piece of art.*

Ridicule consists of words or actions intended to evoke contemptuous laughter at or feelings toward a person. Efforts of someone to find amusement or delight at the expense of another, varying from mere mischief to sheer malice, describe ridicule. Ridicule shows great disrespect by displaying disapproval of who someone is or what they are doing or saying. It is never constructive, but always disruptive. The attempt to embarrass or threaten children out of a habit may work for the present, but is likely to create deep resentment and destroy-self respect.

Some parents mistakenly think that by using certain statements, they are using reverse psychology that will magically force children to try harder to prove their parents wrong. Some sample statements include: "You're too slow to ever make the team." "You'll never make the Honor Roll." "You'll never amount to anything." "You're too little to compete in that contest; no one would buy from you." Parents mean well, but this approach often backfires. Many children will carry their parents' negative predictions throughout life.

Phony Promises

- *When you are older, I'll get you a pony.*
- *If you come with me, I'll give you $5.00.*
- *I'll come home early and take you to the game.*
- *If you are good, we'll go get an ice cream cone.*
- *Someday we'll have lots of money to buy you anything you want.*

Insincere promises made to influence behavior or gain favor can be considered falsehoods. Phony promises wrapped in wishful thinking may be intended only to quieten children or force them to alter their behavior, or to increase your popularity. Even though you may say, "I just wanted to get them to quit crying," phony promises are manipulative through and through. Broken promises have disillusioned many children. Perhaps you have your own stories of unfulfilled promises.

Kids don't forget, nor do they have the perception of time. If you promise to buy your children things or take them places or make "pie in the sky" projections, and then the promises or projections don't materialize, they assume they are responsible, that they don't deserve such attention or opportunities. Never promise anything you cannot provide. Also, avoid making promises too far ahead; the weather or a work schedule may demand a change. Keep promises to a minimum and try to keep them short term to avoid disappointment.

Empty Threats

- *I'm never bringing you shopping with me again!*
- *You touch him again, and I'll break your fingers!*
- *That's the last time I'll ever buy you ice cream in a cone!*
- *If you don't straighten up, Santa won't bring you any presents.*
- *If you don't stop your crying, Grandma will never come to visit again.*

A threat is a statement or other indication of intention to hurt, punish, or destroy. It is an signal that an undesirable event or catastrophe may occur. Most of us have been guilty of making empty threats, especially if we are involved with young children who are not mature enough to challenge our logic. Empty threats are used so indiscriminately in our society, we have to label them the chief offenses with children. Of course, mothers innocently plead, "How else can I get my kids to quiet down and do what I tell them? It's the only way they'll listen to me. I have to scare them."

Empty threats are scare tactics to force children into good behavior or cajole them for bad behavior. They are most often manipulative and not intended to be carried out. Threats to teens that if they do not clean their rooms, they will never get their driver's license or not be allowed to watch TV for a week require more discipline than most of us have in order to follow through. Besides, outrageous statements eventually prove the speaker to be a liar.

How would you feel if your parent drove you by the children's home or detention home regularly and threatened, "If you don't obey, this is where I'll put you?" Many parents have shared such threats with us. Again, trying to manipulate good behavior via threats not only frightens children, it also increases insecurity and creates distrust toward the authority figure. Saying, "Oh, I was just teasing you," does not nullify the fear.

Crushing Criticism

- *Well, son, you managed to strike out. You must feel pretty good about yourself!*
- *Your mind must have holes in it because we went over your spelling words a dozen times. I can't believe you goofed up.*
- *If you can't sing on tune, I suppose it's better to sing loud. I could hear your monotone above everyone.*
- *I can't believe you didn't stand up for me.*

Criticism is censuring or finding fault. It is a close relative to put-downs and sarcasm. Children are easily crushed by destructive criticism springing from deeper motivation such as resentment, embarrassment, disappointment, rejection of attitude, jealousy, or difference of opinion. Accusatory statements such as "you never," "you always," and "you can't" wound and discourage children—and adults. Do you know what it feels like to have a guilt trip put on you?

Blaming, an expression of disapproval, is closely connected to criticism. When children are always suspected of being responsible for infractions, they may suffer forever, like Robert who said: "As a child, I was always blamed for everything, so now I feel guilty and assume everything that goes wrong at home or work is somehow my fault."

A 50-year-old successful businessman told how as a 9-year-old he assisted his father in building projects. His older brothers avoided such involvement.

> *I wanted to please my father in the worst way, so I would follow him around and hand tools to him as he requested and correctly—handle first. To avoid being called slow or ignorant or being cussed at, I tried to anticipate which tool would be needed before Dad would ask for it. My father took great delight in rejecting my tool choice just to prove my foresight wrong.*

You can readily see how this attitude could produce much apprehension and feelings of inferiority in a 9-year-old who tried but constantly failed at pleasing his father. His father's oft-repeated statement still rings in his heart:

> *If I have to repeat it, you weren't listening. If you aren't listening, I don't want you around.*

This type of negative communication may intimidate children to listen out of fear rather than out of respect. Encounters such as these may result in hidden anger that does not emerge for years—usually not until someone is grown and married.

Taunting Teasing

• *Bobby's got a girlfriend.*
• *Don't forget to plug up the drain, or you'll slip through.*
• *I know where you got your cold, by kissing all the boys.*
• *Would you look at those whiskers! Where's my magnifying glass?*

Teasing is annoying someone by making them the victim of irritating remarks or actions repeated time and time again. It is an attempt to embarrass or make another feel uncomfortable or frightened, or to draw attention to an inadequacy or physical weakness.

Since children are bound to receive teasing from relatives and older children, teasing from parents is an overload and really hurts worse. If your children have been teased unkindly, comfort them and do not become part of the negative dialogue. If anyone accepts them for their looks, failures, and inadequacies, it should be their parents.

Lopsided Lecture

• *I'll do the talking; you listen.*
• *No one ever gave me anything.*
• *Growing up wasn't easy for me.*
• *I had to work for my spending money.*
• *Here we go again, you're not using your head.*
• *You don't appreciate the sacrifices we make.*
• *I'm tired of solving the same problem over and over.*
• *When we were kids, we respected what our parents said.*

A lecture is a long and tedious reprimand. Lecturing used to be an accepted discipline method, but do you remember how you felt when your parents or another authority figure lectured? The brief attention span of children often thwarts any benefit of a lecture. "My mind shifts into neutral," a teen said. "Their words go in one ear and out the other," another admitted. You may say everything you know about a subject, but unless your child feels comfortable about listening or has some previous point of reference, excessive information is useless.

Avoid comparing children or their circumstances with siblings or with yourself when you were their age. For the most part, lecturing causes frustration and creates resentment. Kids wonder why their parents do not discuss their problems rather than just expounding, since parents know from experience what a waste of time one-way haranguing is.

Some of you may recall a parent saying in the course of a long rebuke, "You were the biggest accident of my life"; "I regret the day you were born"; "I wonder why God punished me with you"; "We were doing fine until you came along." Children remember little of what you lecture, but they remember whether they felt important or insignificant, smart or dumb, wanted or not wanted, condemned or celebrated. We can say some really dumb things when we are upset and angry or feel insecure.

Children feel stress when they are not allowed to give their side of the story before being accused or punished. We are wise to make it easy for them to talk and admit their mistakes, giving ample opportunity for their perspective. This not only gives our children experience in recalling facts, but it also helps them to express their feelings honestly. If nothing else, insisting that everyone involved in a fracas give their side of the story, whether it is believable or not, reduces tension for all involved.

Interrogation

- *Why do you like him?*
- *What are you hiding?*
- *What's her house like?*
- *Who wrote this letter?*
- *Who was that on the phone?*
- *What happened to your book?*
- *Why don't you tell me things?*
- *Where did you get that money?*
- *How much did you spend on the gift?*
- *Why do you want to go with that group?*

Interrogation, or severe questioning, is closely related to lecture and should likewise be understood and avoided. Some of you surely recall clearly getting the third degree. Clients share how they resented a parent prying into their personal business and badgering them for information.

Did your parents treat you in a condescending manner and with a closed-minded attitude using phrases such as, "None of your alibis!" "That's ridiculous," "Stupid," "Crazy," or "You're out of your mind"? These are guaranteed to prevent open, honest discussion.

Some of us have no idea what emotional pressures our children are under. Often kids will not share their problems for fear we will make light of them. If we do not discuss difficult subjects with our children, they will be reluctant to broach sensitive subjects with us. Young people have shared their idea of unapproachable—angry lectures, silence, disinterest, sour looks, "no" always being the first answer, and absence of hugs and smiles. Do any of these descriptions fit you? If so, try just listening, or smiling. Your children will notice something is different.

Silent Treatment

The silent treatment is the absence of a verbal or emotional response. It is an unnerving, powerful, and manipulative maneuver. Shutting out someone by completely ignoring them is immature behavior, creating more problems and solving none.

"Sometimes my mother's silent treatments lasted 3 weeks," a 40-year-old shared tearfully. "I thought she really hated me. Nothing I did or said ever appeased her. I'll never forget those angry looks."

Certainly you have received the silent treatment from someone. You know its ill effects. Although it is effective, it is unfair. The silent treatment scares children with its unhappy faces and negative body language. Children watch their parents' body language and facial expressions for clues about the seriousness of the situation, trying to determine when the coast is clear. The silent treatment inflicted on children render them helpless with feelings of abandonment. Parental silent treatments are very childish and an inferior, exploitative, and manipulative form of control whether used on children or other adults. Children who are subjected to this method of communication will surely pass it on to the next generation.

Conclusion

Appropriate dialogue with children requires discipline on your part to control rash or thoughtless responses and to protect your children from the inappropriate remarks of other people. Our children respected us for acknowledging and endeavoring to correct our mistakes. Our oldest son, David, said when he was 13, "Mom, don't forget what Haim Ginott said."

We credit Ginott's books *Between Parent and Child* and *Between Parent and Teen* for first drawing our attention to the importance of avoiding inferior family dialogue and teaching us to speak "Childrenese," as he called it. When we read these books, our children were in the 2nd, 5th, 7th, and 8th grades. They eagerly participated in identifying and weeding out flaws—humorous and not so humorous sarcasm, put-downs, and name-calling—that had begun to creep in, robbing our family of the highest quality of respect. By cooperatively holding each other accountable, we accomplished our mission of ridding our family of negative dialogue in about 6 weeks.

We urge you to commit yourself to eliminate senseless, damaging speech from your conversation and in turn to embrace the art of respectful dialogue that equips you to converse intelligently and respectfully with your children—both now and later. Watch these concepts sweeten your relationship with adults also.

TIP #3
Promote diplomatic dialogue.

No doubt you were taught to respect all adults, especially senior adults, regardless of how they behaved or spoke. But that was no guarantee you liked or trusted every adult, was it? Children are fairly good judges of character despite the age or position of the adult. Have you noticed how children initially shy away from angry, dishonest, manipulative, or overbearing adults?

Healthy communication hinges on reciprocal respect between you and your children. We believe it's absolutely essential to teach children to respect authority figures, but the only authentic way to gain their complete confidence and trust is by respecting who *they* are by conversing diplomatically.

Think of an adult relative or friend whom you looked forward to being around when you were a kid. Was it because that person brought you a gift, or because that person noticed you, listened to you, and was respectful of your opinions and feelings?

Because we look for respect and obedience from our children, we may resort to fear tactics and consequently win the battle by force, though we eventually lose the war. Respect and fear are not the same, although they are often linked together. Respect falls into 3 categories: (1) expected respect stemming from ability, achievement, family origin, age, and position; (2) demanded respect resulting from authority, anger, intimidation, and manipulation; and (3) earned respect springing from mutual respect given, selflessness, consideration, and diplomacy.

There are no shortcuts to earning genuine respect. Honest and open conversation with children depends on *earned* respect. Without earned respect for you, your children are less likely to confide in you or accept direction or correction willingly. Alice Miller says in *For Your Own Good,*

> Crucial for healthy development is the respect of their care-givers, tolerance for their feelings, awareness of their needs and grievances, and authenticity on the part of their parents, whose own freedom—and not pedagogical considerations—sets natural limits for children.[3]

As we master the skills of diplomatic dialogue, the earned respect status is sure to emerge. Let's examine some basic guidelines for conversing more effectively with our children.

Before You Speak

Check body language, inflection, and tone. Body language is powerful—narrowed, squinted, angry eyes; pursed lips; tight mouth; clenched jaw; furrowed brow; or clinched fists—the *Look!* frightens children. And the tone of voice conveys rejection or acceptance. The comments "Don't you look nice" and "We can always count on you" can impart criticism or pride, depending on which word in each sentence you emphasize and the tone of your voice, including heavy, hopeless sighs.

Communication consists of 60% body language, 30% voice tone, and a mere 10% verbal content. Are you aware that when we discipline, we make less eye contact, use less than a pleasant tone of voice, and give instructions from a greater distance—usually more than 6 feet away? Our words and instructions take on constructive meaning for our children if we eliminate the element of fear in our dialogue by presenting a positive demeanor.

Understand the level of a child. Get on the physical level of your children—on your knees, if necessary—where you can look them straight in their eyes. Listen with both ears. Touch them when and where appropriate. Try to put yourself in their place.

Prepare them for new experiences by giving due caution toward animals, water, heights, people, darkness, fireworks, carnival rides, haircuts, dentists, doctors, new siblings, flying, crowds, speed, performances, noises, using conversation, reading books, watching TV, and the like. Inspire your children to regard you with respect because you offer them security. Carry an air of genuine concern when you offer protection.

Consider a child's attention span. The attention span of young children is a couple of minutes. As children mature, their ability to focus increases to 10 or 15 minutes. Even adults lose interest after 20 minutes. Subjecting young children to meetings or events geared to adult attention spans brings out the worst in both them and you. When their attendance at adult functions is unavoidable, provide books, paper and pencil, and a piece of candy for a reward—not a bribe. Acknowledge beforehand that the meeting will probably be boring to them. Let them know that you expect and appreciate their cooperation, but then make it as pleasant as possible for them.

As You Speak

Speak on a child's level. What we say is not always what another hears. "I gave you explicit instructions. I said . . ." Sound familiar? We frustrate children when we expect performance or knowledge that is beyond their level, causing them to doubt their intelligence. Stick to their vocabulary. Speak kindly, softly, and firmly. Do not rush their answers; allow them to finish their *own* sentences.

Just as we tend to speak above the level of younger children, sometimes we refuse to recognize the level of teenagers. "Dad still treats me like I'm 6 years old," a 15-year-old female basketball player complained. If you haven't yet heard, "Mom, I'm not a baby! I'm 17; I don't need you to hold my hand," or "Don't you think I know anything? I'll be all right," get prepared—it's normal talk between teens and parents. One parent told his teen, "You don't understand, son, I'm just not sure our product is ready for the market." Allowing a child to grow up can be painful.

Exhibit respect and genuine interest. First, listen politely with interest, openness, and patience. If you have a talkative kid, celebrate her interest, curiosity, and confidence to dialogue with an adult. If she surmises that her questions are respected, she will feel respected.

Allow your children to teach you about some things. Respect their differing tastes, opinions, and dislikes. Listen without criticism or suspicion. Learn to say during a spat, "Here's what I heard you say," to give them the opportunity to correct wrong impressions and prove you were listening. Asking them, "Now what did you hear me say?" teaches them a valuable communication skill.

Listen quietly and uncritically to your children's remarks about what their friends or teachers are saying and doing. Sometimes kids think we are just being nosy, rather than genuinely interested or concerned. We often assume teens are being secretive rather than naturally private.

If your children share information about a friend's inappropriate language or behavior and you retort, "That's it! You're not going to play with that kid anymore!," they will likely cease confiding in you, because the information upsets you and makes you distrust their friends. Children learn early how to protect their friends.

Instead of condemning someone's behavior (in order to let your children know where you stand on the subject), use a nonjudgmental approach: "How do you feel about that kind of language?" "Are you comfortable with someone copying your paper?" "Why do you think Jerry said that to his teacher?" "I wonder why Mr. Smith yelled at you?" By calmly and patiently proposing "I wonder" inquiries and phrasing nonoffensive "how do you feel" questions, your children will not conclude that they are being cross-examined, and you'll discover quite naturally how their morals and attitudes are shaping up.

Coach your children on choosing friends—they're novices, you know. At age 10 our oldest daughter played with a friend who lived with indulgent grandparents. After visits with this friend Kay was belligerent and uncooperative, angry that she wasn't permitted, like Sarah, to have or do "grown-up" things we considered inappropriate. Our guide was, "If a friend pulls you down emotionally, she's too strong, and it's better to limit association." Because we communicated respectfully, Kay accepted the adjustment of "Sarah may come here to play, but we prefer you not go there." This gentle approach provides a simple and workable principle for children to use throughout life.

Communicate praise. We like this anecdote: "Praise is the polish that helps keep a person's self-image bright and sparkling." Affirm the improvement and growth in your children, for instance: "I noticed you hung up your coat." "I appreciate your being quiet while I was on the phone." "Thank you for throwing the paper away." "I appreciate your playing with the baby while I prepared dinner." Don't overdo praise, however.

Older children also respond positively to being appreciated. Some of us are reluctant to praise our own children but willing to praise someone else's. This can transmit the message "I don't like you, but I really like your friend. Why don't you be more like your friend?" This supposed attitude is devastating to children hungering for approval. At least once a day affirm your children for some action or for just enjoying being with them. Saying "I like you," "It's fun to be with you," or "I'm glad we're together" takes little effort and means much.

Communicate individual importance. Children also remember what we don't say—why we never talked to them or asked them questions. Many parents have wept as they said, "My father never told me he loved me," or "My mother never said she was proud of me. I'm still trying to get her approval."

A 19-year-old college student wanted to tell his dad he loved him. He struggled to get up courage to do so at graduation. He was disappointed, though, because after he expended all that energy to say the words, his dad just smiled slightly and gave him a little hug. The question is not whether parents who refrain from verbally expressing their feelings actually *love* their children. Many probably withhold spoken approval because *their* parents did, and they feel awkward speaking in emotional terms they themselves never heard. A 50-year-old schoolteacher surmised:

> *I'm convinced now that my parents really did and do love me. They just didn't know how to give verbal approval when I was younger without fearing they might give me permission to be lazy, dirty, dumb, clumsy, noisy, or bad.*

An era of religious parents believed it was pridefully wrong to express verbal approval of their offspring, leaving many children stifled in self-appreciation. This mother who struggles with very low self-esteem is a prime example: "If I like myself too much, I'm afraid of becoming conceited. That's what my mother always warned us about." How good for her to finally learn that conceit stems from insecurity, not liking herself; and having to feel superior to others, not from accepting herself.

As well as displaying unconditional love for your children, verbalize unconditional love. Rather than saying, "When your room is clean, then I'll love you," or "When you bring home all A's, I'll be proud of you," assure your children you love them first, before they achieve something or look good. It's easy to withhold a smile, a hug, or kind words until you check to see if the chore or responsibility has been completed.

Sometimes we assume that unconditional love means our children are free to do or say anything they please, especially resisting responsibilities. This is a giant step toward permissive parenting. Unconditional love is firm and consistent, accepting the children but rejecting their inappropriate behavior in a gentle, understanding manner controlled by grace. Understanding grace helps us express more patience with our children.

Tease gently. Teasing is a part of life and can build character and also be fun. Gentle teasing says "you are important to me." An old-fashioned inferior idea is that teasing toughens kids and prepares them for the real world. When teasing exceeds the understanding and capacity of children to the point of making them cry or run away, their security has been threatened, and emotional injury occurs.

A Super Bowl winner told how that as the ninth child in his family, his siblings commented on how different he was and speculated that he had been adopted. That insecurity led him to have problems in school and to lack ambition.

It is natural for older children to tease younger children by hiding or throwing their toys, eating their snacks, or pinching or tickling them. Children need to be taught the art of gentle and respectful teasing. If your children cry when gently teased, honor their sensitivity, but help them accept teasing by assuring them, "I'm not laughing at you, but with you." When we can laugh at our own mishaps and acknowledge that something is "a silly thing to worry about" rather than being disgusted with ourselves, our children will learn a marvelous lesson in communicating diplomatically.

Be honest. Don't ask questions when you know the answers. For example, if you find your preschooler's broken toy behind the couch and test his honesty by saying, "Johnny, where's your new truck?" you are being deceitful and paving the way for a lie. He'll probably say, "I don't know." It's better to say, "I found your new truck. I'm sorry to see it's broken." In turn, Johnny will probably tell you how it happened.

Likewise, if you know your teenager did not meet her curfew, but you drill her to see if she will tell the truth, you are being manipulative and dishonest. Saying "I heard you come in at 1:00 A.M., and I'm upset" cuts through lots of hurtful interrogation. Similarly, if you receive confidential information about your children, you can flush out the truth by saying, "I have reason to believe that . . ."

Allow disagreement. The feeling of anger is our helper in identifying issues with our children that need attention. Controlled conflict presents the opportunity to improve relationships. Disagreement is normal, healthy, and builds confidence. Agree to disagree. The more confident one is, the more another is permitted to disagree. Discuss one issue at a time with your children. Keep discussions uncluttered. Disagree respectfully.

Use "I" statements. Using "I" statements is the healthiest diplomatic conversational skill we have found. It creates an atmosphere of openness and respect by removing feelings of control. Learning to phrase requests, questions, or comments into "I" statements requires practice but is well worth the effort.

"I" statements focus on events or viewpoints, as in the following: "I will not permit you to hit Jimmy." "I am disappointed in how you handled that situation." I disagree with your reasoning." "I dislike seeing backpacks on the sofa." "I would have preferred a phone call." "I need time to think it over." When their character is not attacked, children are more willing to correct the situation.

When our youngest child was 8 years old and first heard our new approach, "I get so angry when I see your coat thrown on the couch," he said quickly, "Well, I can fix that." He hung it up.

Instead of telling your children to do something, give them the opportunity to volunteer, such as with these statements: "I need help with . . ." "I'm ready to leave." "I'd like your books put away." "I'm expecting a call and prefer that you not use the phone."

We employ the magic "I" statement approach with our 3 elementary-age grandchildren. If we give the command, "Okay kids, time to go to bed; turn off the television," we usually meet opposition. But if we calmly announce, "I'm ready to give baths; I'll meet you upstairs," and then confidently go upstairs, the kids honor our request.

"I" statements also work with teens. If teens are met at the door with, "Where have you been? You're late! You could have called," an angry response rather than a reasonable explanation is likely. However, saying "I'm glad you're home; I was worried about you" will pave the way for the details of why they are late. This model works well when balancing freedom and curfew.

Avoid directives. "You" directives—should, ought, must, need, or you're going to—are warpath words and come across accusatory, bossy, and lacking in respect. Saying "Your room is a wreck, and you must clean it up before you do anything else" will not get the same harmonious results as, "I expect your room to be straightened up before you take the car keys."

Children usually ignore "you" statements: "When are you going to do your homework?" "It's your turn to scrub out the tub.""You need to empty the trash." They are much more apt to comply when they hear, "I would like for the tub to be cleaned out," or "I want your homework completed before you play computer games."

A condescending statement or question puts children on the defensive: "You know better than that!" "What in the world were you thinking?" But when children hear you say in a controlled way, "I am bothered by what you said or did; I'd like to know how it happened," or "I notice that you are upset," they will probably supply the details. Giving assurances verifies that mistakes do not separate or destroy parental friendship, as with "I dislike what you did, but I still love you,"

Treat sensitive matters with care. Do you remember who told you about sex and reproduction? Was your parent uncomfortable talking about these topics? Perhaps you, too, dread talking to your children about sexual development. Note, your approach is as important as the content. Watch for bits and pieces of the subject from news reports, school assignments, movies, sitcoms, and so on to generate spontaneous teaching moments—one of the best ways to communicate values. Casual questions such as the following provide insight and the opportunity to discuss values: "Did you like what the boy said (or did)?" "What would you do if a kid asked you that question?" "Is that what most kids think today?" Make it easy for your children to discuss any matter with you.

Conclusion

Talking positively to children and protecting them from negative communication is a delightful but responsible challenge because children are eager to learn and grow. Children yearn for parental approval. You have the privilege of helping them to develop a healthy self-esteem through respectful dialogue. Diplomatic dialogue demands discipline, understanding, and growth on your part, but it also earns the right to be consulted—the ultimate desire of every parent.

TIP #4
Adjust your communication style.

- Does the complexity of parenting frustrate you?
- Do you identify with the mom who said, "But, parenting is so daily"?
- Have you said in desperation, "I'd like to ship my kid off for 2 or 3 years. Let someone fix him and return him"?
- Do you ever wonder why one of your children chatters constantly while another remains reserved and quiet?
- Have you turned gray attempting to organize a crisis-motivated child?
- Are you hurt because your child tells you nothing about her activities?
- Are you having a tough time coping with a son who cries easily, or with a daughter who shows no emotions?
- Do you accuse one child of being 7 and going on 3, or another of being 6 and going on 16?
- Are you puzzled by your decisive, "couldn't care less" child who doesn't respond to guilt trips and can function without your approval?
- Does your head swim and your eyes roll while trying to answer your child's endless "why" questions?
- Do you try to respond to your child's numerous reasons and justifications for his actions?
- Do you sometimes feel conned?
- Does it bother you that your teenager talks long and low to unnamed friends, yet won't volunteer an ounce of information to you?

• Are you frustrated with an older teen who has no desire to plan ahead, choosing rather to live just for the pleasures and possessions of today?
• Do you ever feel threatened by one or more of your children?
• Do you yearn to participate in meaningful dialogue with your children, but are unsuccessful in getting on their wave lengths?

Many children tell us their parents, especially their dads, are unapproachable. Some teens shared with us:

Dad sits in his chair behind a paper like an ogre. No smiles. He is very irritable with me. He's so disappointed that I quit football, but I just don't like physical contact.

My parents never ask my opinion or try to find out why I did something. When I handle something a different way than they would, they tag it wrong.

Your child may secretly imagine conversing with you about her hopes and dreams and also hearing yours, but is hesitant to initiate conversation for fear of being misunderstood or compared to another child. Unless and until we learn to truly communicate with our children, that is, exchange ideas and feelings, we'll never really understand them, much less influence them. It is our responsbility as parents to take the lead.

Difficulty in passing on directions for positive living via understandable communication with our children remains one of the most disturbing common problems regardless of linguistic, cultural, financial, social, religious, or educational situation. Since communication and information are closely linked and even used synonymously, we may assume that information offered is automatically communicated. We couldn't be more wrong. All the information available, transmitted over invisible links with unbelievable swiftness and ease, cannot generate or guarantee effective transference.

Communication is much more than conversation. We can avoid verbal pitfalls and be diplomatic in approach, but still fall flat or strike out with certain children. We may read books and articles and attend parenting courses, but still not connect with them. We search for parenting guidelines that will work for the long term—and with every child.

Bridging the Communication Gap

We assume your goals are to rear confident and self-disciplined children, instilling high morals, inspiring a good value system, and teaching responsibilities and commitment. We usually have an idea of what we want our children to know and what direction we want them to go, but few of us possess the natural ability to communicate diplomatically and effectively with every child.

Regardless of how easy it might be to emit information, the real test of how one can effectively use the information is not how well the messages are sent, but how well they are received, because in communicating it is easier to send than receive. How information is heard and received is dependent on the attitude and willingness of the hearer to listen. Most of us need help in presenting understandable messages.

The most dependable and direct way to access meaningful communication with children of all ages is to blend conversational skills with understanding and appreciating individual temperaments and preferences. Just as various flower bulbs require different amounts of light, space, water, and nutrients to produce the healthiest and brightest blooms, so each child has unique needs for understanding and encouragement to become the best person they can become and reach their highest goals. It can be overwhelming to discover that we have several extremely different bulbs to nurture and protect at the same time. If we desire to understand our children's viewpoints and behaviors but do not, we are unnecessarily frustrated, angry, and disappointed.

Understanding temperament preferences often explains what seems like inappropriate behavior in difficult children and wipes out tons of tension. If we differ in temperament from our children, we tend to regard them as difficult rather than merely different. We have more patience with kids who think and function as we do.

You've discovered by experience that a prescribed set of rules or formulas will not work for every home or with every child in that home. What worked on you failed with your sibling. Each family has to determine its particular communication style based on the chemistry of those involved.

Understanding Temperament

Sarah, a 10-year-old, had stomach problems, headaches, tantrums, and academic and social problems. Her room was messy, and her belongings misplaced. She usually forgot instructions. She loved being outside and had imaginary friends. School was too loud and fast, violating her reserved temperament.

Sarah's parents and her sister—who was perfect in her parents' eyes—were very similar in temperament, so they assumed they were normal, but Sarah was not. In fact, they sometimes accused her of being from another planet. Even her grandmother rejected her. Sarah, too, assumed she was weird since she was unlike everyone else in her house and different from her classmates. She was similar to the character in the children's tale the *Ugly Duckling* in which the ugly, unacceptable duckling was really a misunderstood, lovely, graceful, very special swan.

In order to understand and more effectively communicate with Sarah, her parents invested time and effort in learning about and applying temperament information. As a result, they acknowledged that she was radically different from either of them and her older sister. They adjusted the way they talked to her. With affirmation and creative types of chores at home, she received much needed approval. Her teachers began giving Sarah adequate time to complete classwork; she simply could not be hurried. Her gym teacher quit yelling so loudly when Sarah courageously requested that he do so. Her problems disappeared. Now she is a well-adjusted college student pursuing a writing career.

Children respect our endeavors to improve parenting and communication skills. Understanding temperament preferences guarantees more pleasant and fulfilling parenting for you and less painful training for your children.

Before we learned to treat and talk to each of our children differently, parenting was much harder. Even though our children already possessed healthy self-acceptance and were responsible and happy, we weren't confident about teaching them how to accept their differences because we were unaware of God's many unique designs for humans.

After gaining an understanding of temperaments, we learned much about our children. We learned that 2 of our children are primarily facts-and-figures people like their father, and the other 2 are possibility-slanted people like their mother; that our youngest son applies head logic first like his father, while the other children prefer heart logic like their mother. When we understood our children better, we received a clearer picture of the chemistry in our home. Consequently, we adjusted our expectations and released each child to be different from the others and from ourselves. Respect and quality of dialogue improved dramatically. Also, a solution for relieving a fair amount of sibling rivalry distress emerged.

As we blended better communication skills with temperament understanding, inappropriate dialogue and behavior drastically decreased. As soon as we understood and adjusted unfair and/or unreasonable expectations among all of us, tensions were lowered considerably.

Conclusion

Since the temperaments of our children are often the opposite of ours, coping positively can be extremely difficult. The majority of us don't understand our own temperaments, let alone those of our children, and we know even less about how to communicate respectfully to impressionable and/or fiercely independent children. Do you try to make your children obey, assuming obedience is the primary goal of good parenting and can be accomplished by any method of punishment or bribe that gets the job done?

We promise that by blending positive communication skills with knowledge of temperament, you'll more easily gain admittance to the inner world of your children. Seminar attendees send glowing reports of using this approach:

Now that I understand differences in temperament/type and have learned what to say and how to say it, our entire home atmosphere has changed.

Now, I can forgive my child for being different rather than considering him rebellious and rude.

Instead of being upset because my daughter is not interested in the so-called normal teenager interests, I am relaxed and willing to allow her to be different from our other daughter and myself.

We want to help you, too, learn to celebrate differences in your family. We can't emphasize enough that the highest goal for parenting is to encourage children to understand and accept themselves, develop respect for others, cultivate inner discipline, mature spiritually, and become independent. You can help your children achieve these goals by adjusting your style of communication according to the temperament and needs of each child.

TIP #5
Celebrate differences in temperament.

The mother of an 18-year-old daughter and a 16-year-old son commented: "My daughter is extremely sensitive and seems to take herself much too seriously. On the other hand, my son is not bothered by guilt in the least. I have no idea what he's thinking. I just see the results. No one runs over him. My children are mysteries and so opposite. Is it us [parents]? Have we done this to them?"

Janice, the introverted mother of 4-year-old Timmy, was frazzled and irritable much of the time because of his extremely extroverted personality. Janice sighed with relief when she learned in a parenting class that Timmy is legitimately different from her. Timmy is fortunate that his extroverted dad, who can tolerate his noise and endless chatter, manages to spend time with him after work and on the weekends. This arrangement not only rescues Janice but greatly benefits Timmy, providing regular and positive exposure to his father. The alternative over the long term is a resentful mother and a child with potential problems of not accepting himself.

Rose and John Smith are both very much alike in temperament, but their 3 children are all opposite from them and from each other. The children instinctively know that singly and together they are stronger than either of their parents, but when Rose and John present a united front, the children exhibit more respect and experience more security. Because the Smiths have apprised themselves of tempera-ment preferences information and incorporated parenting and communication skills, their young family is flourishing.

Ed Long did not discover until he was 38 years old that clashes with his parents and siblings was primarily a tem-perament problem and could be explained and healed. He assumed his parents didn't like him. Now he realizes that they felt threatened by his extreme introversion. According to Ed, "My love for the abstract, spurred on by my intimi-dating risk-loving spontaneity, was viewed as arrogance, rebellion, and lack of respect. I shut them out without knowing it. I was a complete mystery to my parents."

Before we discuss dealing with different children, think a minute about understanding the person you married. Have you noticed how spouses seem to pair off with their opposites? At 10 p.m. one person comes alive while another folds up. Getting to places early is important to one, whereas sliding in on the bell suits another. Outgoing persons are drawn to their cau-tious and reserved counterparts. Let-things-slide-'til-the-last-minute crises-handlers are attracted to punctual deadline-observers who want to know definitely what's planned. Tenderhearted, please-forgive-me-it-was-all-my-fault softies tend to be intrigued by John Wayne dry-eyed, cold-logic, always-right individuals. And confusion certainly prevails when the guardians of black and white facts attempt to make heads or tails of skip-as-many-steps-as-possible dreamers who have more goals than energy.

Initially, spouses poke fun at temperament/personality dif-ferences, taking them very lightly. Let's be honest. Didn't you secretly project that the person you married would eventually change and accept the wisdom and practicality of your ways and decision making? Most of us voluntarily choose partners whose dispositions, approaches to life, attitudes toward others, and problem-solving approaches are dramatically different from ours—and we may even think superior at first—which explains why our weaknesses often show up as our partner's strengths, and vice versa. It's true, what attracts us in the first place tends to drive us crazy later, especially when we are confronted with the project of parenting. It is not surprising, therefore, that couples often encounter marriage problems when they embark on the task of rearing children.

For some odd reason, we usually find ourselves surrounded by people who think and behave differently from us. Strangely, even biological children are often somewhat different in temperament from their parents. The usual reaction is to label unexpected ideas and behavior as oddities, insecurity, immaturity, inferiority, arrogance, weakness, laziness, snobbishness, or selfishness—all of which upset our level of expectations, produce resentment, and threaten family relations.

God created us to be creatures of communication and growth. A worthy personal challenge is to improve our enjoyment of parenting and to assist ourselves and our children in maintaining healthy relationships. It behooves us, therefore, to acquaint ourselves with God-designed temperament differences, not only to help us appreciate ourselves and cope with our children, but more importantly to avoid resentments by lowering our expectations.

Accepting Our Basic Design

According to the Myers-Briggs Temperament Indicator, there are 16 personality profiles based on 4 broad categories, with each category consisting of 2 distinct preferences. In each of the 4 categories there are 4 temperament code letters, the combinations of which result in 16 different personality types. The categories and temperament codes are listed below. Following are several chapters that elaborate on characteristics of each preference of the personality types as they pertain to more effectively communicating with children in the family structure. Sketches of the 16 temperament combinations are given on pages 98-101.

Social
needing people/needing privacy
(E) Extroversion/(I) Introversion

Information Gathering
relying on facts/relying on ideas
(S) Sensing/(N) Intuition

Decision Making
using head logic/using heart logic
(T) Thinking/(F) Feeling

Lifestyle
preferring structure/preferring spontaneity
(J) Judging/(P) Perceptive

Although we are unique individuals, we each possess a bit of every personality temperament and preference, using each in varying degrees as a particular function or attitude is needed. Of course, we tend to rely on and overuse those preferences that are more natural for us. To illustrate this, write your name in the air or on paper. Now, using the opposite hand, write your name again. The second time felt awkward and required more concentration and time, didn't it? This describes what happens when we are forced to use one of our less developed preferences in responding to a difficult or new situation.

Many times the best response, reaction, or decision will be provided by our less favored preferences, even though it's uncomfortable to use our "other hand." In order to be well balanced, make good decisions, and live a fulfilled life, it's helpful to know the basic differences in preferences and which ones we use automatically, and then strive to develop our less used preferences that add luster, wisdom, and protection to our lives.

Whether we realize it or not, adjusting to opposite temperaments consumes time and energy as we interact with and attempt to understand our children. Spending time and energy in temperament study is a wise investment, however, producing dividends in the present and benefiting our children in the future. When we mix practical communication skills and knowledge of temperament, a climate is created for teaching our children the basics of living and loving. Improvement in handling the challenge of parenting should strengthen all relationships in the family.

By now you may be thinking, "But I'm a single parent. I bear the primary responsibility of my children." Or, "I'm an experienced grandparent." By mastering the skills of communication and understanding temperament, you can eliminate much guesswork and be able to dump feelings of inadequacy.

Dealing with Differences

For the most part, temperament actually determine one's style and technique of parenting. Factoring in children's different temperaments leaves little doubt that accepting everyone's preferences improves harmony and fairness in the home. To this concept of understanding temperament we want to add a coaching approach of parenting. In the chapters about interpretation of preferences you will learn guidelines for dealing with specific, but common, difficulties when your temperament is opposite from that of your children or when one child's temperament differs from that of a sibling.

Learning to celebrate rather than criticize differences transforms potential conflict into unique opportunities for balancing gifts instead of setting them against each other. Although producing friction at times, parental oppositeness in temperament and personality benefits children who quite frequently will be unlike one of their parents.

As you gain expertise in understanding temperament preferences, your own self-esteem will increase. You will respect and appreciate your children more, while also offering them encouragement as they discover who they are and what they really enjoy doing. You will be better equipped to deal with children who may not think or behave like you. Like you, they should be permitted to decide which preferences are their favorites—no clones allowed.

Our goal as parents should be to help our children learn to accept and celebrate their oppositeness from us, their siblings, and their friends. Likewise, we want to coach them to accept and celebrate the temperaments of other people. Keep in mind that mates choose each other, but kids take what they get. When we disagree sharply with our mate, there's some comfort in acknowledging that we initially made the choice, but our children are obliged to accept the parents to whom they are awarded.

Even though they may be biologically related, children in the same family are often painfully opposite in temperament from one or both of their parents and even siblings, with their best option being to adjust and endure. Consequently, some children spend a lifetime sorting out misunderstandings, put-downs, and consequences of unenlightened parenting. The earlier we can apply available knowledge in the lives of our children, the more released and fulfilled our children will be.

Many mental health theorists and clinicians believe that a child's earliest life experiences exert the greatest influence on his or her future personality style. According to Oldham and Morris, "Through our relationship with our parents, we form our fundamental expectations of others and of ourselves. . . . These patterns persist through life within our personality style."[4] Have a wonderful time discovering who you and your children are.

TIP #6
Accept various social preferences.

- Does your child think out loud?
- Do you ever wonder why one child in your family never speaks up and another never shuts up?
- Do you find yourself asking your child, "Are you mad? Are you okay? Is something wrong?"

Social preference determines what people do to you and for you. If being around people drains you, you're probably more introverted. If you draw energy from people, you are probably more extroverted. By God's design, about 25% of the world is decidedly turned inward, having a more natural preference for privacy rather than people, preferring peace and quiet rather than dialogue and disruptions. The remaining 75% of the population is more extroverted, possessing a greater capacity for crowds, noise, group conversations, and disturbances and less need for privacy.

Being totally introverted would be weird, and entirely extroverted obnoxious. Even though everyone exhibits a blend of both introversion and extraversion, each of us leans more one way than the other. Understanding the two social preferences generates respect for each other and makes adjustment more pleasant. This is especially important in a family situation. Consider how knowledge of the following characteristics of introverts and extroverts can help you better relate to your children.

Introversion

Quiet and Patient

Just being in a minority makes introverts special. The world in general seems more receptive to smiling, outgoing children, which often puts introverted children at a distinct disadvantage. Introverts have no choice but to compete orally in our extroverted world. Constant dialogue or noise quickly exhausts the quiet segment, however.

We hear introverts at seminars say, "It really frustrates me when extroverts finish my sentences." On the other hand, they are surprised and amused to hear that their quiet demeanor intimidates extroverts. They comment, "We just assumed that people who are not talking or asking questions knew all the answers."

Introverted children are less likely to interrupt conversations or finish others' sentences. They patiently wait for their turn to talk. At the same time they are more selective and careful with what they say. Because introverts are more reflective, they are likely to make profound statements and draw conclusions rather quickly and succinctly.

After asking an introvert a question and not receiving an instant answer, extroverts often wonder, "Did she think my question was stupid? Is she bored, ill, mad, or just stuck up?" Extroverts are amazed to hear introverts declare, "We're quiet because there's little opportunity allotted for us to speak. By the time we know what we want to say, you guys have moved on to another subject."

Some people assume that less talkative children are merely shy. Not so. Shyness is learned and has more to do with lack of confidence or low self-esteem, which can affect any extroverted or introverted person. It is important to grant an introverted child the gift of ample time to respond.

Reserved and Private

Introverts are reserved and internalize life. Reserved children often choose outgoing friends, knowing instinctively they need a balance. When you acknowledge that opposites attract, you'll be more accepting of your introverted children's assertive, and perhaps noisy, friends. Often introverts say, "I like him because he makes me laugh," or "I don't have to do so much talking." Extroverts appreciate anyone who will listen to them and laugh at their jokes.

Introverts take pride in keeping a confidence, which extroverts appreciate. In turn, introverted children covet confidentiality. If a private conversation or personal information is repeated, children will clam up. Has your child ever shot you the evil eye and scolded, "Mom, I didn't want you to tell Grandma that"? Asking your child "Is it okay if I tell Grandma what your teacher said to you?" will earn you high marks in your child's grade book.

In addition to desiring confidentiality, introverted children value their privacy. They are less likely to share personal matters when several people are listening. Carving out private one-on-one time encourages them to share personal opinions, problems, or experiences. Mixing honest "I" statements with privacy enables introverts to contribute verbally.

"Cindy doesn't tell me anything," a mother moaned. "She has her moods." This could indicate that her daughter is private and has turned her inquisitive mother off. The best way to connect with an introvert is by listening, not lecturing or criticizing. An "I" statement such as "I'm interested in hearing about your evening," is preferable to "What did you do last night?"

Introverted children tend to be especially quiet and perhaps uncommunicative in the morning and after school. The typical early morning hustle and bustle of a family can be difficult for them. Perhaps a time of quietness before other members of the family awaken may be beneficial for introverts. Likewise, they are exhausted after a day of noise, confusion, and disruptions. They probably will not race to answer the telephone or share information. A round of personal questions may make them appear moody or irritable. They need at least a 30-minute recharge after school or being around people. Introverts should be permitted to go quietly to their room after school to listen to music, or go outside to ride their bike, or just be alone and not be bombarded with questions and conversation.

Reserved children are often puzzling and intimidating to outgoing parents until the parents realize that reticence is normal. Avoid put-downs such as: "Why don't you say something?" "People will think you're dumb if you're silent." "Your job is answering the phone; maybe that will teach you to talk." Notice the "you," which indicates lack of respect and serves only to drive introverted children into shyness and promote a sense of inadequacy.

Edit Mentally

Introverts generally think, and then speak, saying exactly what they mean and meaning what they say. On the other hand, by the time they listen, sift through piles of words, and mentally formulate a verbal response, extroverts have either said what their opposites were thinking or changed the subject. "After so long," introverts say, "we just quit trying to get a word in edgewise." Introverts appreciate being invited to share their opinions. Therefore, introverted children need early coaching on how diplomatically to break into conversations, for instance with, "I have something to say," "I'd like to go back to the last question," or "I need time to think." Seeing that this method works, they will gain confidence.

Introverted children are also disadvantaged when grades are based on class participation. Extroverts' hands fly up when questions are asked, whether they know the answers or not. Introverts ponder questions and answer to themselves before volunteering; consequently, they are much too late to be called on. Fortunately, teachers aware of social preferences usually alter their teaching style accordingly.

Dislike Forced Performances

Introverted children find "performance" types of activities to be threatening. Examples include: show and tell in preschool and kindergarten, reading aloud before a class in elementary grades, giving oral reports in junior high, and serving as a committee chairperson in high school.

Similarly, pressuring introverted children to perform before house guests not only violates their privacy but risks creating feelings of inferiority. Invite them to converse or perform, but don't coerce participation. Perhaps singing or playing an instrument for grandma or grandpa would be a good beginning.

Extroversion

Talkative and Opinionated

Extroverted children are easy to spot by their smiles and off-the-cuff remarks. They are not usually questioned about the day's events or how they feel or think because they've already shared the news. Extroverts have a tendency to blurt out what they know. They manage to slide their ideas, comments, and opinions in even though already stated by another. Introverts admire the ability of extroverts to speak quickly, confidently, and extemporaneously, but they wish extroverts would resist the urge to comment on every point made.

Is anyone in your family called "Motor Mouth"? Since talking is as natural as breathing for extroverts, labels such as this can cause extroverts to be ashamed of their God-given preference. Children need to feel good about themselves, not criticized, but they also need to be coached diplomatically to learn to control their volume of words and develop the skill of mental editing. The earlier this type of teaching begins, the easier the expertise is acquired.

Assertive and Confident

One benefit of the extroverted preference is a seemingly inherited dose of confidence. Extroverts take verbal risks by asking questions in public and broaching difficult subjects to get the ball rolling when an awkward stalemate develops. "Extroverts just seem to blurt it out without a wince," an introvert shared. "They never seem to be nervous." But extroverts readily admit that they do suffer from nervousness, but they camouflage their fears with words and smiles. Extroverts are good at "giving it another whirl."

Although extroverted children exhaust introverted parents, as one introverted mother observed, "At least we know what extroverts are thinking or feeling; they're brimming with observations and information." This can present quite a challenge in a house filled with extroverts. Because everyone in our family is extroverted, our youngest daughter used to raise her hand when she was bursting with information and couldn't wait her turn to talk.

Extroverted children usually have many friends, are considered fun, and enjoy popularity at school and with the extended family. People feel like they *know* an extroverted person. You need only to listen, because your assertive child will naturally share down to the minutest detail. Of course, this can embarrass you. Coach your loquacious young children with positive "I" statements: "I'd like for you to be quiet for a few minutes." "I prefer that you listen for a few minutes." "I need to rest my ears." "I'm interested in your story, but now is not a good time for me." Some children are given only two options: shut up or be quiet! A teacher surmised, "If children are not allowed to talk, their hearing is affected." Good coaching avoids squelching children's spontaneous sharing but at the same time encourages them to edit their sharings.

Edit Orally

Ease of conversation more than volumes of words spoken characterizes most extroverts. Yet, extroverts are not always happy with what they say. "It bugs me that I don't know what I'm thinking until I hear myself talk," they confess. They tend to think aloud as if they are trying on ideas and opinions for size. Contradicting themselves in mid-sentence embarrasses them and confuses their listeners. In fact, extroverts have a tendency to speak, then think, and then attempt to straighten out their response.

If you're an introverted parent of a bubbly extrovert, please understand that extroverts can't stop talking completely anymore than introverts can begin to talk a lot. Outgoing people nearly choke on what they want to say; they don't really intend to buy everything they comment about or do everything they say looks like fun. Extroverts *can* train themselves to listen and edit somewhat before they respond, and can even learn to be quiet, especially when introverts are present.

Interrupt Unintentionally

Are you constantly interrupted or your sentences finished by someone else? If you observe conversation for one day, you'll be surprised how common this bad habit is. Teach your children, even the most extroverted ones, to avoid interrupting the conversation of others. Politely, firmly, and softly acknowledge their presence with nonoffensive "I" statements such as "I hear you," or "I'll get to you shortly," rather than rudely saying, "Don't interrupt! That's not polite"—which embarrasses children and teaches them that rudeness is acceptable.

The best teaching is done by example—not interrupting—and by positive statements, for example, "I'm listening to Mrs. Smith," or "Mrs. Smith is speaking right now; I'll listen to you in a minute." Don't make children wait until the entire conversation is finished. After Mrs. Smith finishes her sentence, direct your attention briefly to the child. Some adults merely ignore waiting children, which causes them to increase their interruptions. Children need to be assured that what they have to say or feel is very important.

Unfriendly vs. Overbearing

Introverts are often regarded as suspicious or unfriendly because they do not ask questions, share personal matters readily, or wear wide smiles. Extroverts, on the other hand, are often considered insincere and brash because they do ask questions, unload, and smile.

Extroverts are surprised that introductions, conversation, and attempts to make people comfortable are considered by introverts to be boorish, snoopy, aggressive, forward, pushy, or just plain overbearing. "We mean no harm," an extrovert explained, "We're just trying to be friendly and feel responsible for filling the air waves." Young children can learn to appreciate silence by being discreet regarding personal questions and not feeling obligated to converse incessantly.

Since most extroverts delight in personal interviews, they attempt to draw introverts out as they would like to be drawn out themselves. Introverts will share intimate details only after they know someone well and feel comfortable that what they say will be held in strictest confidence. Extroverts earn the right to hear.

Introverts enjoy and appreciate extroverts' friendliness, easy laughter, and smiles, but they request that extroverts not expect them to duplicate the same. "Just don't assume we are unapproachable or angry because we are sober," introverts plead.

Introverts can learn to smile more and talk more often. Extroverts can function with less conversation. Extroverts who do not take some time to be alone eventually burn out, just as introverts who are not regularly exposed to people are apt to lose balance.

Conclusion

Understanding the different characteristics of social preferences increases appreciation of ourselves and our children and also strengthens our relationships. Making allowances for introversion/extroversion prevents much tension in family relationships and garners respect for the quietest or noisiest member of the family.

Respecting a child's social preference avoids many hurtful comments, put-downs, and problems and also creates an atmosphere for building healthy self-esteem, thereby making parenting much more effective. Since dialogue is our connection to other people and essential to a fulfilled life, if you are sensitive and understanding to the social preferences of your children, you can maintain an integral position in their lives.

***

Now we have an interesting activity for you to put into practice what you are learning in this book. On the following page you will find a sample chart for recording the temperament preferences of your family members. At the conclusion of each coaching tip (#6, 7, 8, 9) you will be given instructions for adding labels to the chart. Information in tip #10 will then help you compile a personality profile for each person based on the letter combinations indicated on the chart.

First, go to the column on the chart marked Social. For each member of your family, mark "E" for extroversion or "I" for introversion. Remember to avoid telling your children they fit one category or the other. Allow them to make their own discovery. Some extroverted children, particularly those who are intuitive, appear to be more reserved and private in their early years.

	Social	Information Gathering	Decision Making	Lifestyle
Adult				
Adult				
Child				
Child				
Child				

TIP #7
Affirm diversity in information gathering.

W hen a job needs to be done, do you first ask "why" rather than "what"? You and your children depend not only on a steady stream of facts and figures to assist with physical survival and daily routine provided by your senses (hearing, sight, smell, touch, taste—the what), but you constantly draw from possibility ideas and strategy to aid in various types of abstract problem solving stemming from intuition (hunches, possibility, imagination, insight, patterns—the why).

Considering the many types of physical and emotional crises, problems, and decisions we face daily, it stands to reason that the same method of information gathering will not suffice in every instance. The medical world describes the different viewpoints rather succinctly: symptoms vs. prevention. Both are desperately needed.

Just as we prefer using one hand in deference to the other when we write, so we discover that one method of information gathering is easier, more natural, or more rewarding than another. Without realizing we're doing so, we may nudge our children into our own habitual ways of information gathering and thereby stymie their full development toward who they were created to be. Children need to be cognizant of both arenas but permitted to spend time pursuing their favorite. Understanding the legitimacy and benefits of differing styles of perception decreases much tension, raises respect in the home, and even provides amusement.

Differentiating between the two methods of information gathering is difficult because initially we are taught survival, that is, to develop physical and practical skills rather than to deal with abstract ideas and possibilities. Also, our senses develop first, whereas intuition—reason, imagination, ideas, design, research —emerges later. The experts project that by 7th grade, intuition as a preferred style of information gathering should be discernible.

The following descriptions will improve understanding of and appreciation for each equally important function and will enable you to identify the most comfortable style(s) for both you and your children.

Sensing

Observable Fact Gathering

Sensing persons are especially gifted at collecting observable black-and-white facts. "Those who strongly prefer sensory information gathering—75% of the nation—discover that their observers are always on. . . . Such people pride themselves on being accurate and exact and are perplexed when others forget the things they can remember so easily."[5]

Because sensing people respect facts, remember facts, stack facts, and expect accuracy—or else someone is lying—they are deliberate about making decisions and require time to process minute details. Sensing people may become overwhelmed when too many facts are presented or several complicated jobs are dumped on them at one time. Sensors are more likely to follow recipes precisely, respect instructions, and proceed as prescribed. As one sensor observed, "I have a recipe for making tea."

Hands-On Approach

Sensing people are usually more dexterous than intuitives. They are proficient in the mechanical, practical, common-sense world and work well with tools, products, and experiences. They hold in their hands their talent and instruments of trade, excelling in products and services and preferring to render physical rather than psychological care. Sensors are more task-oriented, usually preferring to polish a job so they can perform it without mishap.

Sensors are not arrogant by any means. They easily disconnect themselves from what they create or direct or the service they provide. They are content to represent a company, group, or class. Their satisfaction comes from knowing their service or product is helpful, well made, well done, and/or correct.

Creativity and Production

Sensing people generally choose careers that involve products and/or services. For example, they may be teachers, builders, secretaries, doctors, nurses, mechanics, financiers, decorators, or administrators. Sensing workers contribute common sense and practicality to intuitive-slanted projects, chores, tasks, and/or careers. As they get older, sensing people may dabble in several new ventures, but coloring inside the lines describes them well.

Sensing people are more definitive in their creativity. If they are carpenters, they usually stick to the woodworking field and design and improve wood products. When they design a product, say a footstool that suits and satisfies, they have no problem duplicating their product many times over, changing each stool only a little and perhaps putting their initials on each one.

As long as their hands are busy, sensing children are not apt to suffer boredom, whereas intuitives are more likely to become bored with a procedure they've already mastered. Sensing children prefer to perform the same assigned chore daily. They are even likely to become possessive of tasks they have mastered. Because children will most often select jobs that parallel their temperament, a sensing teen would probably enjoy washing the family car because it is dirty, whereas an intuitive teen would more likely volunteer to have it presentable for a date—same job, different reason. Sensing children like to be shown a method; intuitive ones prefer to invent their own method and may use a different one each time they work.

Observing sensing and intuitive siblings working together is quite revealing and amusing. Sensing children frequently accuse the less mechanical crowd of being lazy dreamers and inventing ways to avoid manual labor, and complain that they do all the grunt work. Intuitives defend, "We'd rather work smart using our minds to avoid getting our hands dirty." Intuitives assume brainstorming is as much work as stacking wood or running the vacuum—and they're right.

We are likely to violate our children by assigning exclusively one type of chore or duty completely out of their league. Recall the 58-year-old man referred to earlier whose father gave him a hands-on project simply because he thought a 10-year-old should be able to accomplish it. When the boy fouled up, the father showed his consternation by saying, "I'm so ashamed of you, I'm not even going to tell my friends you are my son." The father was probably a sensing person and became quite frustrated dealing with a non-hands-on intuitive son.

Knowing whether individual children are primarily sensing or intuitive assists you in assigning chores and projects that appropriately train and tactfully challenge them to develop a variety of skills. Healthy survival requires a blend of both styles. Sensing children reared in predominantly intuitive homes exposed to analysis and ideas may experience balance in their lives, but they'll always prefer the hands-on arena. Sensitive parents parcel out both types of projects, explaining to children that we profit from doing things we dislike in order to be well-balanced and prepared for adulthood. We need to coach children to try many things and assure them they can do anything they want to do whether or not it falls securely into their tempera-ment preferences.

Past Experience

Sensing people tend to trust past experiences. They balance today by looking at yesterday, preferring to handle problems as they encounter them. Do you say, "Let tomorrow worry about itself," while your counterparts engage in questions, projections, and predictions of what's going to happen or what they're going to do years down the road?

Sensing children become overwhelmed and frustrated when reminded of too many future events or responsibilities. They do better with a day-to-day schedule. Sensing people like to fit in with society and tradition, are closer to and more comfortable in the conscious world, and are tagged the creature-comfort crowd because they are mindful of the heat, cold, empty tea glasses, maps, flashlights, money, credit cards, and so on. Sensing people major on hosting, making sure everyone is cozy and all systems are running. Since sensing children accept and even enjoy the mundane, intuitive parents and older siblings need to be cautioned against taking advantage of their serving disposition.

Repetition

"We've always done it that way" is a favorite sensing expression. Repetitive action and routine appeal to sensing people and contribute to their security and self-worth, while keeping the physical world around them stable, comfortable, usable, affordable, neat, and organized.

Most sensing children/teens respond to a regular schedule and function better when given time to assimilate information or when forewarned about changes. Have you noticed that your children resist constant change? Sensing people easily form habits that may last a lifetime. If you phone your sensing children after they arrive home from school at 3:00 for three days in a row, they'll expect a call at the same time every day. If you are late making the call, they may want to know why, even though you never decided on a particular time.

Sensing parents are likely to consult the past for pointers about parenting. They tend to use "when I was your age" reasons for rules and regulations. True, experience is a good teacher, but it is not our sole instructor. Since the coaching approach using temperament preferences is relatively new, sensing children will require extensive examination. You may need to violate your own preferred method by consulting the opposite way in order to set good examples for your children and to accommodate their style.

Focused Conversation

Conversations centered around events and experiences in common and a rehearsal of who, what, when, and where in chronological order describe a sensing person's easiest and most enjoyable conversation style. They have difficulty interviewing others extemporaneously, preferring to rely on a guide of possible questions.

Because sensing people prefer to discuss one subject at a time, allow sensing children to rehearse the myriad details and describe the events of their day hour by hour without breaking in with questions or impatient sighs.

Intuition

Unprovable Possibilities/Analysis

Persons who gather information through possibility thinking, hunches, design, and "what might be" are more alive to the unknown world—like the absent-minded professor—leaving little room or time for mundane facts, figures, and practical concerns.[6]

Intuitives make up approximately 25% of the nation, a minority not easily understood, but nevertheless a special group. This segment of society mentally weighs evidence and possibilities, perceiving things as they *could* be or as they *want* them to be. Although intuitives may be regarded as having their "head in the clouds" when it comes to hands-on projects, they can see clearly around corners, read between the lines, and spot a phony.

Because intuitive people respect ideas, analysis, and unprovable abstract facts, they are comfortable predicting outcomes. Intuitives' possibility/analysis is helpful in creative and constructive disciplining of children—a balance to the sensing parent's conventional mode. Remember, opposites attract, so having both intuitive and sensing parents is quite possible, although most parents will share the sensing preference. When sensing parents rear intuitive children, or when both parents are intuitives, special understanding is needed.

Intuitives can project excellent solutions to abstract problems but may not be able to produce hard facts and figures to show how they arrived at their conclusions. They trust their hunches and vibes. Also, because intuitives at times have difficulty recalling black-and-white details, they often tangle facts from several events in an effort to answer questions.

But because sensing parents insist on accuracy, intuitive children are often suspected of being deceitful and untruthful. Anyone can lie, but intuitives get blamed more often because they genuinely can't recall the fact-by-fact fall of events. They are imaginative, so are capable of and guilty of exaggerations, embellishments, understatements, and dodging the entire subject.

In a firm, diplomatic, and consistent manner, we need to help intuitive children sort out the truth and stay with the subject. Separating fantasy and reality is one of the greatest challenges an intuitive faces.

Theory and Brainstorming

Why? Why Not? How Come? These are three favorite inquiries of intuitives, who are in a constant state of brainstorming.

Theory appeals to intuitives' complex minds equipping them for research, engineering, counseling, systems analysis, problem solving, writing, or theology—to name a few career options. Do you have a 10-track mind, always thinking about something else while you're involved in a routine task? This is one reason intuitives lose their keys, books, and glasses. "It's not lost," they say, "I just can't find it."

Is your child concerned about reasons behind the facts—always striving for the big picture? Intuitives tend to skim facts they regard as insignificant, or they grasp two or three facts and proceed. Skipping steps is a common intuitive urge and drawback. Sometimes, though, it works—and saves time!

Intuitive children are likely to ask 20 questions regarding someone else's proposal. As intriguing facts are presented, their minds go skittering ahead, considering how that knowledge or principle could be put to use. Consequently, they sometimes miss subsequent facts and data—such as homework assignments—not because they are disinterested, but because they are preoccupied. Intuitives will stumble over facts in reach of a goal. "My goal is to have a goal, or 4, or perhaps 9," an intuitive explained. Without several goals, intuitives wither. Propelled by time pressure, they thrive on having more to do than they'll ever accomplish. Their personal challenge is, "Let me show you that I can do the impossible."

Often children aren't consulted because of their age, but intuitives have wonderful ideas and solutions to offer. If you consult them, you not only access invaluable resources, but you also contribute to the children's self-worth. Intuitives *are* their ideas. Convincing intuitive children to consider black-and-white facts before they jump to conclusions requires patience and ingenuity on your part but yields balancing benefits.

Creativity and Production

Working with their hands does not bring intuitives the satisfaction it does to sensing people. Unless their intangible offerings of ideas, solutions, and designs are recorded on paper, displayed on canvas, acted out, or presented in lectures or music, their lives have limited meaning.[7]

Intuitives tend to be creative in many unrelated areas such as music, art, gardening, photography, and writing. Many say they wish they were extremely adept in just 1 or 2 areas rather than partially skilled in 5 or 6. Learning to focus is a chief goal and dream of intuitives.

Teach your intuitive children how to focus, accepting the fact that no class or after school job will be totally satisfying. Intuitives prefer to deal with the unknown, preferring the challenge of searching for the pieces to the puzzle of life. They can hardly resist getting involved in analyzing a personal or systems problem any more than sensing persons can resist repairing a broken object or counting the cost. Intuitives would rather replace a broken object (cost is usually the last consideration) because they're not very good at repairing things. They can learn, but it's always a struggle. We harm intuitive children by comparing their ineptness at repair to a sensing child who is a whiz at fixing things.

Intuitive children become extremely bored with routine procedures. They want to move to a higher level of responsibility when duties are too easy and don't demand their ingenuity. Because intuitives are so easily bored with repetitive endeavors, they prefer a variety of chores, tasks, and assignments. Regularly raking leaves or dusting furniture becomes so boring that thoroughness is sacrificed. Rotating tasks and granting more responsibility appeases intuitive children.

As adults, intuitives are likely to flow from job to job until they dub themselves a "jack-of-all trades" and "master of none."

Those who do remain in sensing type jobs bring their creative "big picture" improvement ideas to the workplace, which often intimidates sensing people. Intuitives tolerate hands-on jobs by creating head games or setting personal completion goals.

Because intuitives are interested in behavior and why things happen, they easily think up questions to ask and enjoy problem solving. Seeing the big picture, many are drawn to careers in the field of counseling, fine arts, research, design, analysis, writing, strategy, and computer technology.

Intuitives reared in strictly sensing homes directed toward hands-on assignments may develop mechanical abilities, even though they will attempt to camouflage the boredom by devising their own methods. Therefore, many intuitives don't discover until midlife that the intuitive arena is actually their most authentic and enjoyable source of perception.

Reputation and Recognition

Image is of utmost importance to intuitives. They want to succeed not merely for grades or wealth, but for the recognition of reaching goals and enhancement of reputation. Intuitives crave to be important; they yearn to be consulted.

Because intuitives are committed to growth, improvement, and change, their natural inclination is to point out the imperfect—which they do fairly consistently, earning them the "flaw-pickers" award. Intuitives are amazed and disillusioned to learn that others perceive them as critical or negative when their motivation is betterment. It is true that intuitives are usually the ones who stir the pot. They have to learn to live with imperfection and accept situations that cannot be improved. Intuitives prefer recognition for their ideas rather than commendation for a good job. Actually, intuitive children are natural perfectionists. They try to be flawless and want their families to be perfect. They are very embarrassed when obvious mistakes are mentioned. They prefer to correct blunders smoothly, quickly, and privately.

Analytical Conversation

Conversing with intuitives can be confusing because they love to theorize, analyze, and rationalize, constantly hungering for new ideas and information, able to discuss several subjects at once. They prefer to make a point and then elaborate on it rather than give all the details before opening the discussion. When they recount their day, they'll probably begin with the most exciting part and relate it as a saga building to an exciting conclusion. Intuitives categorize events rather than chronicle them.

Because intuitives have so many ideas—not always wild—running through their minds, they do not always finish sentences, can't remember what they just said, or do not hear your answer, leaving the impression that the "lights are on, but nobody's home." But as one teenager said, "Oh, somebody's home; I just can't find the door!"

Because their conversations are steeped with information, analysis, questions, observations, suggestions, or solutions about how someone, something, or a system could be improved or changed, intuitives are often pictured as arrogant "know-it-alls."

When asked a question, intuitives usually feel obligated to give an answer—hoping it's right. They watch the listener's face to see if their answer is accepted. Their ballpark answers or projections are often right on target or pretty close. Intuitives are expert "guesstimaters."

Intuitives prefer conversation about ideas and facts they've never heard before. "If I don't learn something as a result of a conversation," an intuitive explained, "I feel like I've wasted my time and mind." Intuitive children are likely to intimidate a sensing parent unintentionally with difficult questions and profound observations, for example, "What makes lightning?"

Futuristic

Intuitives dream about tomorrow, next month, next year, or 10 years hence, and have the distinct ability to project what might happen without having experienced a sample situation. "I know what's going to happen," they say with all confidence. Sensing parents often conclude that their intuitive children are either psychic or pretentious. Sometimes parents, siblings, and acquaintances call them smart-alecks. Intuitives can't help their skill in looking ahead. They like to design their lives, and actually worry more about tomorrow than today.

Intuitive children have a different style of playing because of their ability to project with vivid imagination. They prefer play-acting and made-up games and often use toys (or the boxes they come in) in their acting or games. Sensing children prefer traditional games such as playing house or school and are more likely to use toys for the intended purpose or for mimicking real life.

I have seen this evidenced in my grandchildren. My sensing grandchild has a difficult time getting her older intuitive brother and younger intuitive sister to include her in their games because she prefers traditional games while her siblings prefer playacting Star Wars and imaginary saga games. Once she finally convinced them to let her join their game. She was involved only a short time, however. I commented to her, "I thought you were playing with the kids." "I was," she sighed, "but I got killed off right away."

Intuitive children find life to be somewhat difficult, especially when they are small or in the minority among relatives or in a classroom. Most intuitives we counsel admit apologetically that they suspect they are a bit weird because they can or want to see into the future. They feel much better about themselves, however, when they learn they have plenty of company.

Conclusion

Sensing children are easier to parent unless you yourself are intuitive. They do not like a lot of changes and can handle the repetitious segments of life. But be careful not to make them feel inadequate, inferior, uninteresting, or stuck. They need help to celebrate the fact that more people are like themselves.

Highly intuitive children present a tremendous challenge. Coach these complicated "bulbs" to accept how they've been programmed. Celebrate their differences, but encourage them to purposely consult their less preferred hands-on capabilities. Give intuitive children more incentive, time, and encouragement to complete boring jobs.

The world is more exciting because of these opposite arenas, each needing the other's input. We all have to accept that no one gets to do 100% of the time what we enjoy the most. Functioning in our opposite arena builds character.

***

Now turn to the chart on page 54. Under the arena of Information Gathering, mark "S" for sensing or "N" for intuitive for you, your mate, and each child. If you're not sure which is your favorite method of information gathering, you're probably intuitive—since sensing people usually know without a doubt. Knowing your preference will help you give close attention to the other arena. Our intention is not to expect you or your children to become equal, but to be knowledgeable enough to benefit from resourcing both preferences. Neither arena is superior or inferior.

Again, do not be dogmatic about which preference you think your children are. We want to avoid labeling children who are still in their formative years. Just knowing the probabilities and possibilities provides insight into parenting. Remember, all of us are a blend of preferences.

Honor different paths to decision making.

Which do you say the most: "I've got to have harmony" or "I want to do what's right"? Both head logic—having harmony—and heart logic—doing what's right—influence our decision making. Persons who make "head" decisions based on cold facts emerging from a logical basis are referred to in this study as *thinkers*. Those who make "heart" decisions based primarily on emotions stemming from values are designated as *feelers*.

The world seems to be evenly divided between thinkers and feelers. However, roughly 40% of men prefer to use heart logic, and approximately 40% of women are more comfortable using head logic. This produces much disparity in our world as logical females struggle to use their feelings and softhearted males grapple with trying to be tougher. Our family is not evenly divided in this preference. Our youngest son and his dad are thinkers, and the rest of us are feelers.

For overall social development and stability, we occasionally need to exercise and blend both methods of decision making even though one method is easier to use. Learning to consult the opposite option requires daily practice.[8]

Thinking

Aspire to Be Right

Head-logic decision-making is based on cause-and-effect practicalities and situation-based choices involving cold, hard facts rather than emotions. Even though feeling decision-making develops first, natural logical decision-making can be detected in many young children—which surprises feeling parents. I remember the insistent statement of my 4-year-old grandson when I kept exclaiming about finding my lost purse: "Grandma, it's *over!*"

Thinking children are more likely to declare bluntly, "I'm not going" rather than expressing the feeling, "I don't want to go." Logical deciders generally don't elect to ask others for their opinions before making a decision. Until they are shown limitations in their facts or flaws in their ideas, they're likely to stick to their decisions.[9]

When I (Jim) was 12, an aunt very close to our family died. I couldn't understand why everyone cried and cried but me. She had been ill for a long time and was better off relieved of her suffering, I rationalized. When asked if I were going to the funeral, I said, "No, I want to remember her like she was." (I'd heard someone say that once.) Attending her funeral wouldn't help her in any way. My parents didn't challenge my decision because they were used to my practical approach to life. But that was a bad decision, and I needed emotional facts. They should have made me go out of respect and support for my 11-year-old cousin who had become an orphan and would be coming to live with us. Now I realize I was the only thinker in the family, including my parents, and I've regretted that decision to this day.

When our youngest son—a thinker—was just a little guy, rather than asking if he could ride his bike here or there, he just went. Instinctively, he didn't need parental approval to do things he considered perfectly reasonable. Our oldest son—a feeler who always asked permission—accused us of allowing Roger to have his way because he was the youngest. The truth was, we didn't find out until afterwards what Roger had decided to do without permission. "I don't have to get permission when I know my decisions are right," Roger defended. These situations demanded firm reminders: "What you did was not wrong, but not letting us know where you were going was inconsiderate. Therefore, no bike riding for the rest of the day." This was good discipline, not punishment.

Thinkers—both male and female—make most of their decisions based on concrete facts, and do not feel guilty if others disagree. That's why they can argue one minute and be snoring the next, even though feelers may still be crying. This also explains why thinkers can make a decision and stick to it unless supplied with additional facts that might change the rightness of their decision. "I'd rather know that my decision was correct than agreeable with everyone," a thinker said. Thinkers feel rather sorry for anyone who disagrees with their accurate decisions and want others to "own" their perceptions, ideas, and opinions. Thinkers, unlike feelers, do not connect one decision emotionally with another. Thinking children are often regarded as uncooperative.

Arbitrary, unannounced decisions commit feelers to thinkers' decisions unless feelers object verbally in logical ways. If a feeler disputes a thinker's decision, the thinker might have regrets but not guilt. "Why am I responsible for someone else's feelings?" a thinker would ask. Thinkers are more likely to experience feelings of inadequacy before feelings of guilt.

Value Trust and Respect

The greatest gift we can give thinkers is trust and respect for their judgment. Usually their decisions are made for the welfare of the ones they care about in the name of convenience, economy, and other practical considerations. But because they lack understanding about the underlying emotions and expectations of feelers, their decisions come across as self-centered, callous, and without much warmth.

Thinking children need assistance in learning to be warm and cooperative and considerate of others' suggestions. Unless logical deciders are coached to appreciate the feelings of others, they can become authoritarian, stern, and unapproachable. They will intimidate softhearted feelers and alienate themselves from family and friends.[10]

Thinkers trust their own judgment and expect approval from others. "I don't need approval before I make a decision," a thinker shared, "but I'm bothered when my child criticizes my decisions, unless I can be shown where my judgment was wrong."

Thinkers assume agreement is evident if they are not questioned. Therefore, feeling decision makers are wise to risk making waves by confidently and tearlessly expressing to thinkers what they like and dislike before a decision is finalized. When verbalizing a different or emotional perspective, feelers must be committed to resist being intimidated by thinkers' brief, often terse defenses. It takes two feelers to balance a thinker. Also, feelers should not assume that thinkers can or care to read their minds. Thinkers pick up hints with their eardrums. They need information to be pointed out and underlined; and then they need to be reminded.

Most thinkers dislike long, involved explanations. Some feelers, even male feelers, admit they are somewhat afraid of their thinking counterparts, which can create major communication hang-ups. In order to gain respect from thinkers, feelers are forced to implement the cold logic style, even though it makes them feel mean or selfish. Sometimes feeling parents are fearful of thinking children.

Parents and teachers are both surprised and impressed as they observe the development and courage of young thinkers. To illustrate this, we'll use another story about our youngest son, Roger. He and a friend, both teenagers, were responsible for a fire in the woods one fall. In discussing the incident, he shared what punishment his friend was given, so we figured we should follow suit: withdraw some privileges and teach him a lesson. So we asked his opinion about what he thought would be fair discipline. Roger related his feelings about the situation:

> *Well, Mom and Dad, we didn't start the fire on purpose; it was an accident. We were scared, but we helped put it out. I've got burns on my body. I've already learned a lesson, but, if it would make you feel better to punish me some more, go ahead.*

What would you have done? Roger's reasoning made good sense to his thinking dad, so we dropped the subject. But we have gotten lots of mileage from it. Roger is not only a thinker but also possesses persuasive, analytical, intuitive abilities—the strongest combination.

Conceal Emotions

Because thinkers rarely cry and have a tendency to get mad first and then hurt, some feelers assume thinkers have no emotions and are immune to hurt feelings. Some even accuse thinkers of having no heart or perhaps ice in their veins. Thinkers *do* get hurt, especially if their judgment is not trusted and respected, but their emotions are often concealed and controlled. Because thinkers do not normally feel sorry for themselves, take things personally, or experience the depths of false guilt and hurt feelings that feelers do, they are not expert at understanding others' emotions. Feelers are wiser to patiently inform thinkers about their emotions rather than fault them for not being sensitive.

Thinkers have a difficult time giving what they don't expect from others, especially affirmation and approval for completed tasks. Their arms reach to their backs—automatically giving themselves approval. "I don't expect everyone to thank me for going to work every day. Why should I thank you for carrying out the trash? It's your job!" Even so, thinking children and teens like to be told that their parents and other significant adults are proud of them.

If your children make decisions through impersonal logic, they are equipped to think through hurts and put-downs and then put them aside—what feelers struggle all their lives to do. Thinkers are able to soar over problems, thus avoiding the mud and mire because they deal with facts and logic, not feelings and emotions. They prefer to speak straight and simply, whereas feelers are more likely to grovel through the puddles and under barbed wire to seek approval and a solution. The goal of logical deciders is not harmony or approval, but to make the best decision in order to get the job done. They'd rather not hurt your feelings, but if they are convinced their decision is the best, hurt feelings, disagreement, or tears won't budge them.

When disciplining thinking children regarding inappropriate behavior, address them in their favorite language of cause and effect. Avoid lecture, berating, or attempting to conjure up guilt feelings. Appropriate language would be, for example, "What you did/said is inappropriate and unacceptable to us and will not be tolerated because . . . We want you to go to your room for 10 minutes and think about these things, and then we will discuss how to resolve the problem." Don't assume that if there are no tears or physical punishment, you have failed. Metering out discipline with respect for your children builds their self-respect and confidence. They may not automatically see consequences; they rely on you to respectfully point out inconsistencies and infractions.

Relating to Thinkers

If you are a feeler involved in a tug-of-war with children who prefer the thinking preference, remind yourself that when you feel a little bit mean or selfish, you are about right. What should you do when a child won't take your word for something? For instance, how do you convince a 4-year-old not to drink hot chocolate at a ball game when you know it's too hot? Do you give in to avoid a scene and embarrassment by saying, "Okay, find out for yourself!" and allow the child to burn his/her tongue? Will giving in convince the child you are right, or will it make a child not trust your protection?

You could sweet talk a feeling child into waiting, but you must deal differently with a thinking child. Give the child a choice, for example: "I understand that you want the hot chocolate right now. If you insist on having the hot chocolate now, it will be poured out. If you find patience to wait, you'll get to drink it. I will either pour out this hot chocolate that would burn your tongue, or you will give it time to cool. You make the choice. Have it later or not at all. I'll give you several minutes to think it over." The principle is: acknowledge a thinker's viewpoint before giving your own; acknowledging an attitude does not condone it. You can also reduce tension with feeling children by demonstrating respect and assuring them you have listened to their side. This also buys time to think.

Have you fallen into the trap of trying to compel your thinking child to be sensitive, insisting that she display remorse at hurting feelings or offending others? Because their feelings rarely get hurt, thinkers are really not aware of how their honesty comes across as bluntness and thus wounding feelers. The best advice for dealing with thinking children is to read their lips and understand that for them to say things with great warmth and tenderness requires special energy and focus. They are often less demonstrative and usually resist hugs and kisses from mom and grandma, but please don't take it personally. The head-logic crowd is surprised when feelers want them to affirm their love or check to see if they still want them to go with them. Their stance is, "I told you once, and I haven't changed my mind."

A grandmother relates the following experience she had with her 10-year-old thinking grandson.

I scolded him so severely for hurting a younger sibling that he cried. That was the first time I'd ever seen him cry for something besides a physical accident. Then, I received more information that revealed I had not heard all the facts. I went to his room where he was still sniffing and apologized for jumping to conclusions before I had all the facts. "I hope we can just forget this happened, Ron," I pleaded. "Will you forgive me?" He assured me he forgave me and that we'd forget about it. When I saw him the next day, I said, "I'm still feeling badly about my scolding you yesterday." "Grandma," he said, "I thought it was over!" I'm relieved and impressed with his use of logic.

Thinkers hate to sound wimpy. They avoid statements such as "Would you please . . . ," "Do you mind . . . ," and "I hate to bother you, but . . ." On the other hand, thinking parents belittle feeling children for being overly sensitive and shedding tears easily, and feel obligated to teach them to be tough. "Big boys don't cry" is no longer an acceptable guideline. Big boys who are feelers *do* cry, and it's okay because it's normal. Many grown men seek therapy today because their feeling decision-making preference was resisted by their fathers. Many thinking adult women also struggle with self-doubt stemming from cruel criticism in childhood because they did not fit the feminine rationale.

Coach your thinking children to be diplomatic when dealing with the other half of the world, to practice being approachable and kindhearted, and to deliberately invite and consider the input and opinions of others. Adults who wield the strongest influence are those who teach thinking children to respect and appreciate the feeling temperament preference of others. Thinkers can learn to develop warmth and emotions to a point, but usually they need constant, respectful reminders as they strive to consult their soft side and meet the emotional needs of others.

Feeling

Devoted to Harmony

Heart-logic decision making is sensitive to the feelings of others. Feelers want to maintain peace and harmony, and avoid being criticized or hurting someone's feelings. Feelers, great with diplomacy, gift wrap their requests or regrets: "I hope you don't mind," "Please don't take this personally," I hate to disappoint you." Feelers often say "yes" when they mean "no," which can leave a residue of resentment and unhappiness.

Because feeling children instinctively are people pleasers, wise parents can coach them to confidently express their down-to-earth, honest opinions and learn to accept disharmony, disappointment, and disagreement as normal and okay at times. Feeling persons of all ages need to learn that being honest is not synonymous with being selfish, and that constantly meeting the expectations of themselves and others can lead to serious co-dependency problems. Feelers need to learn that genuine harmony means everyone has had equal opportunity to be heard and to be honest—in other words, "agree to disagree."

Feelers say what they think others want or expect to hear in order to promote unanimity. Feelers' reactions to compliments may vary from feeling guilty—if they know they did not do their best—to wondering if the flatterer is saying what they think the person needs to hear or taking the compliment with a grain of salt.

"The desire for harmony at any cost, guilt over displeased people, disappointment at not receiving thanks or appreciation threaten the emotional decider's self-esteem. They cannot respect themselves unless others respect them. This is opposite of the logical decider's inborn self-respect."[11]

The people-based decisions of feelers, although not always making sound financial or logistical sense, are in many situations the warmest, wisest, and best decisions because maintaining peace and harmony and being concerned for some-one's feelings is extremely appropriate, especially in a family setting affecting a child's self-esteem.

Seek Approval First

Feelers want everyone to be satisfied and in agreement. They function best when they receive approval from several others before they make final decisions. They are greatly influenced by the number of opinions for or against.

Feeling children need encouragement to stand up for their choices despite disapproval and doubt from others. They need to hear, "It's okay if you choose something different than what we or others suggest or expect." Feelers have to be trained to trust their own tastes and opinions.

Feelers have to learn to convert thinkers' actions into love they can measure. Feelers like to know that significant people think and care about them. Being remembered on special occasions ranks very high on their expectation list. Birthday celebrations are more important to feeling children because they rely on others to initiate approval. Whereas many thinking children have to be reminded when special days are drawing near, feeling children need to learn that it's not wrong (but smart) to remind thinkers.

Feelers often feel faulted for having a problem, especially when they receive responses from thinkers such as, "That's ridiculous," "Why would you let a little thing like that bother you?" or "Why did you let that happen in the first place?" Therefore, feelers are reluctant to admit certain differences in opinions or share problems. Without realizing it, thinkers tend to make light of feelers' problems and inefficient solutions. Rather than acknowledge the legitimacy of feelers' outlooks and encourage them, thinkers may question that problems even exist or may criticize the "impractical" solutions of feelers or "beat around the bush."

Desire to Be Nice

Feelers would rather be warm and considerate than right. Sometimes people think feelers are nicer than they really are because feelers operate out of guilt—false guilt. Avoiding guilt or bad press encourages feelers to smile when they feel like crying, continue working when they'd rather quit, and sacrifice when they have exceeded the limits. For this reason, feeling children can easily be taken advantage of because they are easily persuaded as they try to keep everyone happy. Usually thinking children do only what they want to do or see a good reason for doing, so it is more difficult to take advantage of them.

Feelers hurt when forced to make unpopular decisions. Thinkers counter with, "We don't enjoy making unpopular decisions either, but it's got to be done." But because feelers connect emotions with decisions, their hearts receive many bumps. They are afraid that disagreeing with or not doing what someone has requested will threaten their friendship. They want everyone to like them, even the people they don't like. This is one reason so many feelers get picked on. Thinkers wisely advise feelers that it's impossible to make one decision that will please everyone. Therefore, feelers should not fault themselves when others are unhappy with their decisions. Likewise, as a feeling parent you should consult head logic so as to protect your heart and remain consistent and firm when children put undo pressure on you to change your final decision.

Relating to Feelers

Not much has been said regarding preschoolers, but since the feeling preference develops first, a word about whining can help readers with small children. Young children, especially around the age of 2 or 3, will resort to whining as a lever to get your attention. They will nag for positive attention, but will settle for negative attention such as scolding. Usually their unconscious goal is your *total* attention. Children know that nothing is worse than being completely ignored.

Keep in mind that there is a cause for all behavior. Therefore, take whining seriously in order to discover the cause. Study the pattern of the whining. Is it before, during, or after a nap? Is it when you're on the telephone, paying bills, or visiting with a friend? Is it when other children are coming home from school? Is it when the child is sleepy, hungry, or bored?

Ignore whining but not the whiner. Don't reward whiners by doing what they demand. You've taught them how to get your attention, even if you qualify your actions and object by saying, "This is the last time," "I can't stand your whining," or "I'll be glad when you get over this phase."

Stay abreast of a child's insecure behavior. Statements such as "Before I put you down for a nap, I want to hold you," "Let's read a couple of stories before the children come home from school," or "I brought you a glass of water in case you need a drink" teaches children they do not have to whine to get your total attention. Give children brief, total attention before they demand it. Kindly explain: "I understand what you want, and when I hear no more crying or whining, as soon as I can, I will . . ." Let them know what you plan to say or do. Always keep your promises. If children continue to whine after you've given them positive attention, ignore the behavior. Speak to them about another subject.

Longer-than-usual eye contact, a firm "No," and an accompanying disapproving look to toddlers should take care of most minor mistakes. When children reach the age of 3½ or 4, briefly explain the reasons behind your rules and limits. If the discussions are lengthy, children may use dialogue as a means of demanding more than their fair share of your attention or of challenging your expectations and thus your authority, which will destroy their security if they succeed in frustrating you.

Feelers suffer deeply from being ignored, disrespected, slighted, or shut out—all feelings of inferiority. Feelers regard absence of positive feedback as criticism. Their feelings are not always based on actual intentions or opinions of others, but rather on assumptions. Along with what is and isn't said, feelers read faces, eyes, body language, and tones and assume everyone else can and does. When feelers understand that thinkers are not as expert as they are at reading body language and interpreting sighs, then they can eliminate many injured feelings.

Since feelers are likely to give themselves approval only if others do, they are constantly testing their worth. Feelers need to hear "I love you" and also receive smiles, hugs, and other signs of affirmation. Thinkers declare that if feelers continually say "I love you," they question whether or not they meant it the first time. Their position is, "I said it once, and when I change my mind, I'll let you know." Verbal affirmation to feelers is what vitamin C is to our bodies—a fresh, dependable supply is needed daily.

Feelers like to be appreciated for who they are and the kind things they say and do. Both males and females need the 6 "A" words: appreciation, affection, approval, attention, acceptance, and affirmation. The twin principle to "It's difficult to give what one does not need" is, "It's difficult to withhold what one likes to give." In other words, feelers like to receive approval and therefore attempt to give it to thinkers who don't appreciate it all that much.

Thinking parents are often surprised to learn that their soft-hearted teenage sons also need a regular dose of appreciation and affirmation. Thinking people regard appreciation as something to be earned and not awarded just to make someone feel good. For example, a thinking parent might say, "If you do a good job or make a common-sense decision, I will appreciate what you've done."

Feelers struggle constantly with feelings of hurt and guilt that contribute to low self-esteem. But when they finally realize this is normal, they admit the truth and teach themselves to think through situations and to accept themselves.

Learn to acknowledge your sensitive areas and express your emotional needs to thinkers, without tears and apologies. This sets a good example for feeling children. When thinkers learn how important it is for feelers to be affirmed, they learn to give affirmation. Feeling children need encouragement to become relaxed with thinking parents. A feeling daughter cringes when a parent, often a father, is all business and gives the impression she is infringing on his time or is disappointed in her. "Get to the point," a parent might insist sternly, tossing a feeling child into a whirlwind of rejection.

Without finding out why his 9-year-old softhearted son was crying, a thinking father reacted with automatic disapproval by responding sarcastically, "Did someone die? Did you lose a leg?" He taunted his son by throwing up his arms and pretending to cry. (Many thinking parents assume that laughing at boys who cry will toughen them up and make them stop being sensitive. However, that method boomerangs and gives boys problems later on in accepting and liking themselves.) Hearing this ordeal, the boy's mother calmly and kindly drew out what was troubling her son. Then, behind closed doors she confidently and candidly expressed to her husband her disapproval of his immature and negative reaction and prevailed upon him to respond differently in the future. This required courage on her part because she was intimidated by him.

Softhearted parents who buffer children from a thinking parent—"Don't let Dad or Mom see you do that"—often create an underlying fear toward the less sensitive parent. Protective parents become conductors, with everything going through them. Eventually, thinking parents will accuse feeling parents of turning children against them.

Affirming children for who they are and for appropriate behavior is of utmost importance for healthy emotional development, but especially for those preferring feeling decision making. The more children are affirmed for appropriate behavior, the less you will have to deal with inappropriate behavior.

Conclusion

Since the world is split about 50/50 in the decision-making arena, we need to acquire healthy respect for both options. Of course, it's not easy to consult our opposite tendency. Celebrate your children's God-given decision-making preference by coaching them to develop the opposite preference.

***

Once again turn to the chart on page 54. Under the category Decision Making, mark "T" for each thinker and "F" for each feeler in your family. Keep in mind that the feeling preference develops first, so some thinking children will show many characteristics of their feeling counterparts. Resist the urge to say to a child, "You are this way or that way." Allow children to discover gradually their favorite preference, which may not happen until they reach 7th grade. You should observe improved and warmer home dialogue as you apply this information.

TIP #9
Embrace variety in lifestyle approaches.

- *Now I know why I never make my bed.*
- *No wonder I wait until the last minute to write my papers.*
- *I now know why my sister is so bossy, but I can't hold it against her anymore.*
- *All this time I've been blaming my mother for not being able to rest until all my work is done.*

As with other temperament indicators, opposite lifestyles seem to attract. Structured persons eager for closure are willing to make a decision and then change it if necessary. Spontaneous folks prefer to let options remain open until the last minute and then make only one decision. Sometimes the structured segment fear that the spontaneous crowd doesn't intend to make a decision. These extremes can be most frustrating on the home front.

Lifestyle preferences can be amusing to distinguish, and also very freeing. It's important to be able to laugh about our differences and admit that we all require lots of acceptance and forgiveness. After all, celebrating differences is our aim.

According to John Oldham, writing in *The Personality Self-Portrait,* personality lifestyle is like a map of our inner geography and the outward direction of our life. We follow its pathway everyday. The development of our personality style depends on nature and nurture, heredity and environment.

Understanding our individual needs for either spontaneity or structure can provide immediate release for dealing with children who are gifted with the opposite inclination from ourselves. Initially, children may use their natural tendencies as excuses or justification for their "annoying" behavior; but eventually, they will accept themselves and work to establish balance in the home. As with the other categories, it's normal to switch back and forth between arenas depending on the situation.

The following interpretation of lifestyle preferences will help you discern the dominant trait of both you and your children, and thus put you on the path toward more effective communication. Although it is based on the Myers-Briggs Temperament Indicator, instead of referring to preferences as judging or perceptive, for the sake of clarity we use the terms structure and spontaneity.

Structure

Schedule/Prepare

- *My lists have lists.*
- *I feel lost without a watch.*
- *I can't live without my calendar.*
- *I don't use lists; I have notebooks.*
- *What are we going to do after we get home?*
- *I get so mad with myself if I forget anything.*
- *Oh, good, a free day! Let's plan something to do.*
- *I always allow extra time just in case something happens.*

Scheduling and organizing events, working the plan, and anticipating the outcome give security to structured persons. Taking mental or physical risks lack appeal. Improvising is undesirable, since surprises may cause embarassment.

Structured children will get ready ahead of time—even the night before—for school or a trip. They are likely to check their book bags twice to make sure everything is packed, including an extra pencil. You really don't have to teach structured children to keep their things together; it seems to come naturally to them.

Structured children are fairly predictable because their psyches run by the clock. They enjoy a schedule and like to know ahead of time what they will be doing or where the family is going. They feel violated when plans change abruptly. Perhaps you have a child who balks at doing something on the spur of the moment. Some structured children even need to be prepared for ending an event.

If you are a structured parent who likes to follow a schedule, and you have a child who is more laid back, you need to learn to relax, be flexible, and roll with the punches when situations change or plans don't work out. Similarly, if you dislike making advance preparations and sticking to an agenda, but your child functions well with structure, you need to make adjustments in your lifestyle. Remember, when you model for children the attitude you desire, your teaching is validated.

Begin/Finish

- *Let's go.*
- *Hurry up.*
- *Don't waste time.*
- *We're going to be late.*
- *Get your work finished.*
- *We don't have enough time.*
- *I have to finish this before I can go.*

Structured persons live according to beginnings and endings. The finish is most important. Structured children may begin an assignment immediately and not rest until it's finished. They'll tackle unpleasant tasks first because they love to scratch items off their lists. They have no objection to picking up toys, closing doors, or straightening up. Structured children are more likely to play with one toy at a time and then put it away before using another. They become frustrated when their playmates gather and then mix all their books, cars, or dolls.

Work/Play

• *Give me 15 minutes to finish.*
• *How many minutes until we go?*
• *I want your chores done right now.*
• *Before you go out to play, pick up your toys.*
• *As soon as I finish the dishes, I'll read you a story.*
• *After you use the scissors, be sure to put them back.*
• *You've got to go to bed early so you can get up early.*
• *I've got to finish my paper tonight; it's due next week.*
• *It's 5 minutes after 9 o'clock; you're late for your bedtime.*
• *You can bounce your ball 5 more times, but then put it away.*

"Work, it must be done" is the motto for structured people. "Work *is* my play," they defend when someone faults them for being workaholics. They identify with the old Chinese proverb, "A man who likes his work never works another day in his life." Structured people even have a way of turning free time into work with detailed preparations, plans, and provisions made in case of emergencies. They have to purposely arrange for being spontaneous.

Relaxation and play do not come naturally for structured children. They may choose to do their homework before they relax, and may even miss a game or party to finish assignments or to work ahead. They often vie for more time than necessary to finish an assignment because they do not work as well under pressure. It's imperative that parents understand the difference between the work and play of structured sensing and structured intuitive children.

Structured sensing children are more patient in completing repetitious jobs, whereas structured intuitives are easily distracted from repetitious physical labor. Structured intuitive children need several unrelated and challenging jobs on their list, perhaps working on a couple at the same time. For example, structured sensing children would enjoy cleaning out the silverware drawer and putting everything back, but structured intuitive children would be more likely to redesign the contents and clean out the drawer in the process. The task is accomplished, but with different motivation and methods.

Structured sensing children like method and organization. They will follow a suggested method. On the other hand, structured intuitives may give the suggested method a try, but prefer designing their own. For example, structured sensing children will line up all their cars according to size or color, while structured intuitives will organize their toys by category—pickup, sedan, van. Knowing the legitimate differences in approaches opens up a new world of understanding and accepting behavior.

Structured children usually do not object to a list of chores since they feel a sense of accomplishment at the completion of tasks. In addition, they enjoy the praise they receive after jobs are finished. If they are respected, they respond well to directives.

We need to check our priorities so that work doesn't take precedence over relationships with our children. Teaching them the work ethic is important, but we need to balance our "listaholic" tendencies by prioritizing quality demands on our time. All work does not have to be finished before having fun. A free day is excellent preventive medicine and a good example.

Direct/Boss

• *Why don't you be "it"?*
• *Someone has to take charge.*
• *Let's get started, or we'll never get back.*

• I'll tell you in plenty of time when we're ready to begin.
• You make the sandwiches; I'll get the other stuff together.
• You fill the trucks with sand, and I'll drive them to the sand pile.

Because of their organization and desire for closure, structured persons inherently become the managers of the world. They can take orders or give orders. Because they make plans and give instructions, they can be overbearing without realizing it. If no one else is in charge, they assume responsibility. They run into trouble, however, when they attempt to organize spontaneous workers and tell them what to do. They encounter opposition in the form of "You'll never organize me, only irritate me."

Bossy people do well to employ diplomatic dialogue skills such as making nonoffensive and less domineering "I" statements. Much tension is produced when structured children try to supervise and organize spontaneous parents. The children become frustrated when their parents give no directives or set no physical priorities or limits. Structured children like to keep rules. Perhaps you are a spontaneous parent who has difficulty giving detailed direction to your structured children who crave boundaries. What should you do? Accept the mandatory crossing into another arena. Allow school and community schedules to pressure/help you to be more time/completion conscious, even though you may grow weary of functioning this way.

Spontaneity

Crises/Surprises

• I like to rescue.
• I like surprises.
• I never wear a watch.
• You're not imposing on me.
• I work well under pressure.
• I do my best work at the last minute.

Spontaneous people don't like tight schedules, so they don't stick to exact appointment times. Responding enthusiastically to the present need or enjoying what is happening to the fullest without regard to time energizes them. They prefer minimal planning; therefore, they won't be disappointed if plans don't materialize. The unexpected is exciting. Spontaneous people also handle emergencies well, including middle-of-the-night needs, and they won't quit until the emergency is over, even if they miss meals and sleep. They major on crises and excitement.

Although the structured work world complete with time clocks, bells, rules, and appointments violates the spontaneous segment, persons of this nature must learn to tolerate a certain amount of rigidity to be part of the program. Schools are primarily sensing and structured, so spontaneous teachers are usually popular because they are laid back and make their classes fun—a breath of fresh air for the spontaneous who had rather be outdoors.

But alas, school rules violate the spontaneous types. When the last bell rings, they're still on the playground. They hate to stop doing what they enjoy in order to start a new, inside assignment. They prefer the word "project" as opposed to "assignment"—it sounds more free and fun. They long for recess. Spontaneous students at the junior high and and high schooler levels hang around the doors of the classroom and then slip into class at the very last minute. They hate to sit and wait for something to begin.

Initiate/Procrastinate

- *Expect me when you see me.*
- *It's still 3:00 until it's 4:00.*
- *Always allow me 10 extra minutes.*
- *Whew! I made it, just in the nick of time!*
- *Two things I hate to do—get up and go to bed.*

• *I know where everything is; I just can't tell you.*
• *Why put something away if you're going to use it again?*
• *It doesn't take much sleep for me; besides, I'm afraid I might miss something.*

The words "play," "initiate," "fun," "outdoors," "later," and "unstoppable" describe the spontaneous mind-set. Spontaneous people are gifted in initiating projects. They exude ideas and possibilities for having fun and finding solutions for impossible jobs requiring risk taking, whether it's skydiving or responding to a mental or physical emergency. But interest wanes when the process turns monotonous; procrastination results. Because they are unconcerned with deadlines and keeping things in order, they sometimes create a crisis in order to motivate themselves into action. Spontaneous people actually become organized when they have an emergency or little time to accomplish their tasks.

Spontaneous children typically have problems with organizing their time and belongings and also completing projects, both at home and school. Allow them to suffer consequences when they're young. For instance, if they sleep late and then want you to rush them to school, don't. Have them receive the school's discipline for tardiness. When they lose their book or forget their gym bag or homework time after time, allow them to receive the deserved demerits. It is better that they learn difficult lessons while they can be coached tenderly, yet firmly, by loving parents to be on time, consult a calendar, and keep up with their belongings. They need to understand that employees who have not learned self-discipline are judged harshly and lose their jobs.

To motivate spontaneous children, instigate a race, use a time watch, or offer a prize or an outdoor privilege. Provide them with white markerboards or fun calendars for recording activities, chores, school assignments/projects, and music or sports practices. Help them to complete tasks by encouraging them along the way with affirmation and praise, remembering that finishing doesn't accomplish for the spontaneous what it does for the structured.

Play/Process

- *I'll help you clean up your room.*
- *I did it backwards, but I finished first.*
- *I don't mind the work if I can see a difference.*
- *I'll vacuum as long as I hear something going up the handle.*
- *There's no need to clean up as I go; I'll wait until I'm finished.*

Spontaneous adults usually work in spurts and prefer the night shift. They are attracted to rescue-type occupations such as emergency room personnel, paramedics, police work, crisis counseling, open-scheduled positions, operating big machinery, and acting. They often work at night or take advantage of bad weather for mundane inside work. When the sun is shining, they like to be outside.

Similarly, spontaneous children enjoy the process associated with various activities that may be considered work, for example: picking up someone else's books and papers after a collision in the hall, rearranging the classroom before the bell rings, helping someone change a flat tire, running track, playing ball, wrestling, and participating in chorus or drama. If spontaneous children are allowed to choose a certain number of chores from a list and are given a long deadline to complete them, they'll do the fun jobs first—the ones they consider play—and finish the others at the last minute. They also respond to impromptu stimulation such as, "Let's see how fast we can clean up your room."

Spontaneous children especially like to play outdoors or do anything that doesn't have to be completed or put away. Inside or outside work combined with an exciting process is incentive enough. Yard work appeals to them because the yard stays neat for a few days, unlike a house or room.

Spontaneous children seem to irritate structured parents because they resist detailed instruction, do not like to begin right away, are easily side-tracked, and may not finish on time. Since our world system honors finished projects, clean rooms, and completed papers, spontaneous children often miss out on important affirmation and praise because finishing monotonous projects is difficult and/or brief deadlines catch them unaware. We need to praise them while they are in the process of completing chores and assignments not only to encourage them, but to teach them the value and necessity of finishing. Acknowledge that doing routine tasks is a less fulfilling struggle. Guide them toward exciting careers.

Indirect/Journeyer

- *We'll see about it.*
- *Don't fence me in.*
- *We'll wait and see.*
- *I lost track of the time.*
- *I'll be home in a little while.*
- *I don't want to be in charge.*
- *Who made you boss over me?*
- *Don't worry; I'll make it somehow.*
- *Wearing a watch just makes me nervous.*

Not only do spontaneous people dislike receiving orders, they do not clamor to be the boss. Spontaneous parents usually fall into the permissive camp, giving their children too much time and too many options. In an emergency they can run the show, but that's not their preference.

Spontaneous children and teens are often difficult to parent because they are unpredictable and strong-willed. They tend to dislike authority and to be impatient and short-tempered. Yet, if we respect their temperaments and patiently and diplomatically coach them in maintaining composure and developing patience, they will cooperate.

Spontaneous children need a certain degree of action and freedom. After a long week in school, they don't want an organized weekend. But, according to Alice Miller,

> This does not mean that children should be raised without any restraints. Crucial for healthy development is the respect of their caregivers, tolerance for their feelings, awareness of their needs and grievances, and authenticity on the part of their parents, whose own freedom—and not pedagogical considerations—sets natural limits for children.[12]

Spontaneous children do appreciate help with setting priorities for getting a task completed. They relax when they are aware that their parents understand how difficult it is to function in a structured world. Acknowledging a problem does not condone it, but it reduces friction so that other options can be considered. Effective communication requires patience, diplomacy, and time.

Conclusion

Although opposite lifestyle preferences cause anxiety in a family, with one member pushing and the other resisting, we desperately need both at designated times. Negotiation and compromise are key words for families to live in harmony. We can learn much from each other.

***

You are now ready to complete the temperament chart on page 54. For the arena Lifestyle, mark "J" for structured members and "P" for the spontaneous ones in your family. Because intuitives lodge in the perceptive world, structured intuitives possess many spontaneous characteristics, making it difficult to ascertain whether they are structured or spontaneous. The desire to finish or have closure usually reveals the preference for structure. All children—sensing and intuitive—exhibit more spontaneity until they reach 6th or 7th grade, or until they are released to be who they really are.

TIP #10

Emphasize the uniqueness
of personality types.

*In some ways you are like some others. In some ways you
are like no other. Be the unique you God has designed and
wants you to be.*

We trust that as you have read about the various temperaments in this book, you have recognized the preferences
of yourself and your children. We suggest you share the explanation of temperament preferences with older children and teens
to enable them to distinguish their own preferences. Only they
can identify their God-designed preferences, although through
close observation you can venture an educated guess based on
their frequently-used behavior patterns as young children.

Once again go to your family's chart. Make sure you have
recorded each member's temperament preference using the
following guide.

E Extroversion	**I** Introversion
S Sensing	**N** Intuition
T Thinking	**F** Feeling
J Judging	**P** Perceptive

Now combine each family member's 4 letters. Look at the following personality profile sketches that list the qualities of
particular letter combinations. The sketches emphasize the
uniqueness of each personality type, even though there will be
some overlapping of preferences. While avoiding labeling family
members based on your own observations, select the profile you
think best describes each person.

Myers-Briggs Temperament Indicator

Introversion/Sensing (IS)

ISFJ—Servers
private and/or quiet
want provable facts
/hands-on experience
resist radical changes
lead with heart logic
seek approval
need harmony
want acceptance
organized
work to the finish
respect and follow rules
take or give orders

ISFP—Sympathizers
private and/or quiet
want provable facts
/hands-on experience
resist radical changes
lead with heart logic
seek approval
need harmony
want acceptance
impulsive
play is the process
respect but bend rules
dislike giving or taking orders

ISTJ—Conscientious Workers
private and/or quiet
want provable facts
/hands-on experience
resist radical changes
rely on head logic
expect approval
want trust and/or respect
organized
work to the finish
respect and follow rules
take or give orders

ISTP—Unstoppable Operators
private and/or quiet
want provable facts
/hands-on experience
resist radical changes
rely on head logic
expect approval
want trust and/or respect
impulsive
play is the process
respect but bend rules
dislike giving or taking orders

Extraversion/Sensing (ES)

<u>ESFJ—Hosts and Hostesses</u>
open
outgoing
want provable facts
/hands-on experience
resist radical changes
use heart logic
seek approval
promote harmony
want acceptance
organized
work to the finish
respect and follow rules
take or give orders

<u>ESTJ—Organizers</u>
open
outgoing
confident
want provable facts
/hands-on experience
resist radical changes
rely on head logic
expect approval
want trust and/or respect
organized
work to the finish
respect and follow rules
take or give orders

<u>ESFP—Performers</u>
open and outgoing
want provable facts
/hands-on experience
resist radical changes
use heart logic
seek approval
promote harmony
want acceptance
impulsive
play is the process
respect but bend rules
dislike giving or taking orders

<u>ESTP—Rescuers</u>
open and/or outgoing
want provable facts
/hands-on experience
resist radical changes
rely on head logic
expect approval
want trust and/or respect
impulsive
play is the process
respect but bend rules
dislike giving or taking orders

Introversion/Intuition (IN)

INFJ—Empathizers
private and/or quiet
see possibilities
trust vibes
battle boredom
pursue challenges
set goals
use heart logic
seek approval
promote harmony
want acceptance
structured
work to the finish
question but follow rules
take orders/prefer to delegate

INTJ—Expert Strategists
private and/or quiet
see possibilities and reasons
battle boredom
pursue challenges
analyze systems
set long-range goals
rely on head logic
expect approval
want trust and/or respect
structured
work to the finish
question rules
establish own procedure
delegate if necessary

INFP—Idealists
private and/or quiet
see possibilities
trust vibes
battle boredom
pursue challenges
analyze behavior
handle emotional crises
use heart logic
seek approval
promote harmony
want acceptance
play is the process
unscheduled
impulsive
question and bend rules
dislike being in charge

INTP—Think Tank Experts
private and/or quiet
see possibilities and reasons
battle boredom
pursue challenges
handle systems' crises
rely on head logic
expect approval
want trust and/or respect
play is the process
unscheduled
impulsive
brainstormers
resist control
crave freedom
prefer not to be in charge

Extraversion/Intuition (EN)

ENFJ—Encouragers
outgoing
bubbly
assertive
see possibilities
trust hunches
analyze behavior
10-track mind
battle boredom
pursue challenges and/or goals
lead with heart logic
seek approval
encourage harmony
want acceptance
structured
work to the finish
question and adjust rules
follow orders
delegate

ENFP—Catalysts
outgoing
bubbly
assertive
see possibilities
trust hunches
analyze behavior
battle boredom

pursue challenges
/emotional crises
use heart logic
seek approval
encourage harmony
play is the process
impulsive
question and massage rules
crave freedom and action

ENTJ—Head Chiefs
outgoing
assertive
confident
see possibilities
trust reasons
analyze systems and behavior
battle boredom
pursue challenges
set long-range goals
rely on head logic
expect approval
want trust and/or respect
structured
work to the finish
question rules
establish own procedure
assume they are in charge

<u>ENTP—Powerful People Movers</u>
outgoing
assertive
confident
see possibilities
trust reasons
analyze systems and behavior
battle boredom
pursue challenges
handle systems' crises
rely on head logic
expect approval
want trust and/or respect
play is the process
impulsive
crave freedom and action

Conclusion

Don't you wish your parents had known all this when you were a kid? Improving parenting is so easy and initiates positive cycles that will benefit generations to come. Taking the next lap in blending differences may be the most revealing and exciting for you.

TIP #11
Respect differences between siblings.

Now that you have identified the personality types of your children, hopefully you can better understand the dynamics in your family. Clashes between temperament types can be very severe among siblings. Your response to this rivalry can enhance or hamper communication with individual children.

Intuitive children reared with sensing siblings may suffer from feelings of physical inadequacies. Because they prefer abstract involvements and are not as adept with their hands, they may resist doing boring physical work—which sensing siblings often refer to as lazy endeavors. On the other hand, intuitives may not respect the hands-on talents of their sensing siblings. Either scenario can lead to intense sibling rivalry.

Sibling rivalry generally stems from several sources: age difference, the pure form; parental preferences, the avoidable root; and temperament preferences, the genetic factor. The closer children are in age, the greater the rivalry. The most intense rivalry occurs when children are about 1 year apart, and drops off progressively after an age spread of 3 years.

Showing Favoritism

Many children who suffer from low self-esteem discover the source of rivalry to be jealousy toward a sibling who seems to be more talented or better accepted by a parent. Unintentionally, we parents tend to "play favorites" among our children based on the following criteria:

- looks
- neatness
- actions
- academic ability
- athletic ability
- musical ability
- peaceful
- smiles a lot

- quietness
- entertaining
- cooperative attitude
- enjoys work
- not argumentative
- has friends
- birth order

The perils of parental favoritism are depicted succinctly in the biblical story of Joseph. Joseph's father gave him a coat of many colors, denoting special privileges because Joseph was the offspring of his father's favorite wife. Joseph's favored position cost him dearly. Like most children, Joseph didn't ask to be favored; he merely responded to attitudes around him. Chances are, he may have had a more pleasing temperament and personality than his brothers. Perhaps his father did not understand and/or accept the differences among his sons. Joseph found that being favored was a burden when compared to the embroiled resentment that surfaced later in his life.

Affirming Differences

Rather than gravitating toward certain children, and thus adding to sibling rivalry, we need to affirm each child for his/her individual and unique contribution to the family. Some ways to do this are:

- Avoid comparing one child to another.
- Try to understand the temperament of each child, thus increasing sensitivity to individual abilities and knowing when and if to give praise for performance or ideas.
- Give each child chores and projects that fit them and in turn helps build their self-esteem.

- Teach siblings to allow their opposites the right to prefer certain types of activities.
- Avoid the tendency to intervene in every negative interaction between siblings. Give them time to work things out in an appropriate manner. Your job is to see that no one is mistreated physically or emotionally.
- Teach siblings to disagree respectfully, intelligently, and constructively.

Sibling Rivalry

Despite our best efforts to accept and affirm sibling differences, some rivalry is inevitable. We should not be overly concerned with sibling competition, however. Arguments and disagreements are good training for life in the adult world. We need to maintain a proper perspective. Remember, a sibling relationship is only one of many factors that influence developing children. A little competition doesn't spell disaster. Children need to learn to negotiate with each other. When they are not allowed to oppose each other, they lose something in their development.

Children learn important negotiating skills when they feud. It may be a very natural context in which they can argue and then learn how to resolve conflict. For instance, in fighting over the last piece of cake, allowing one child to divide it and the other child to choose first will keep things fair and square. Negotiation requires time but is a valuable teacher and naturally redemptive.

Sibling rivalry often continues into adulthood, but siblings who have strong positive ties with each other maintain those ties through the years. Helping our children understand *why* they are having disagreements and *how* they can compromise and respect each other will guarantee them a chance for a long and happy friendship.

Case Studies

The dynamics among siblings and between ourselves and our children are powerful. We can encourage positive relationships by respecting the individuality of each child. Using the labels indicated in the Myers-Briggs Temperament Indicator, the following case studies reflect the complex dynamics in family systems and also offer solutions for blending different temperaments within a household. Although the traditional family unit is used for simplicity and clarity, the same principles apply to other family situations such as single-parent, blended, extended, and so on.

The Wilsons (ISFJ/ENFP/ENTP)

Amy (ISFJ), age 13, is a good student and has one close friend. She spends much time in her room reading, making crafts, and playing with her kitten. Amy says she hates her brother Billy and refuses to associate with him. She is irritable with the family and selfish with her possessions. "I can hardly wait to leave this rotten home," she threatens.

Billy, age 10, is noisy and constantly pesters Amy. He gets into her "things," but no one seems to care.

Shirley (ENFP), the mother, is disheartened by Amy's unhappiness, disappointed by her selfishness, and hurt by her negative attitude toward Billy. Shirley wants harmony. She also loves conversation and excitement and can tolerate noise. Housework is not a top priority with her, so the house is cluttered unless company is due. Mealtimes are erratic. Phone calls and friends always come first because Shirley has a difficult time saying no to anyone who has a personal problem or need. She has a tendency to let mundane chores slide and often stays up late getting caught up.

Fred (ENTP), the father, sees no reason for Amy to be intolerant, unhappy, uncooperative, and irritable. "Lighten up and be a positive part of the family," he lectures. Fred, a successful field representative, is an avid golfer and enjoys gardening and being outside. Always on the go, he is a late nighter with many projects pending. He is impulsive and impatient and dislikes having to wait or deal with trivial matters. Fred is a last-minute person who works well under pressure.

Evaluation

Introversion/Extroversion. Amy, an introvert, is violated in her extroverted home because confusion, rushing, noise, and disruptions irritate and drain her. Her family's frequent questions, comments, and criticism about her lack of friends and desire for privacy give Amy an inferiority complex. Amy's "antisocial" behavior concerns her parents.

Sensing/Intuition. Shirley and Fred, both intuitives, wonder where Amy learned to be so sensitive about the condition of her room and belongings; she didn't get it from them. They regard her fussiness as insecurity or an unhealthy attachment to her belongings. They do not put the same value on physical things. The Wilsons fear that Amy has an emotional problem.

Thinking/Feeling. Feeling types like Amy dislike confrontation and tend to bottle up stress. When pushed or irritated beyond their limit, they often retaliate with hurtful comments or silent treatments. Fred and Shirley admit that they often tease Amy about her "worrywart ways" and fail to give her the affirmation and approval she needs.

Structure/Spontaneity. Because Amy is very structured, she likes to anticipate events with ample time to finish what she is doing, straighten her room, and get ready. Her parents are spontaneous and prefer the process rather than planning or finishing. They like surprises and dealing with emergencies.

*Clashing temperaments is the primary source of dysfunction in the Wilson family. Unbeknown to her parents, Amy is being disrespected. She is completely opposite from her dad and only like her mom in one area—feeling. Amy's type is actually more common than Shirley's or Fred's, but because of the chemistry of this home, Amy has been blamed for the problem.

Blending

In therapy the Wilson family had a great time discussing their temperaments. Fred and Shirley quickly recognized that the family's noisiness, busyness, questions, and criticisms frustrate and intimidate Amy and are unfair. They now respect Amy's differences as legitimate, and realize her need for privacy is normal and not something she should overcome. They have accepted her small cadre of friends. Billy was fascinated with information regarding innate behavior and was willing to adjust his actions on Amy's behalf. Fred and Shirley have slowed the family dialogue pace to fit Amy by waiting for her to volunteer information.

Fred and Shirley now show understanding for Amy's instinctive need for schedule and organization by trying to adhere to a family time schedule. They cooperate in keeping clutter under control since it means so much to Amy. They resist the urge to make those "drop everything, let's go" trips, and endeavor to give Amy some advance notice. When Amy understood how extroverted spontaneous people function, she lowered her expectations of her parents and Billy—which also lowered her resentment level.

To help them learn to appreciate each other, the Wilsons have scheduled times for playing board games together as a family. They take walks and work in the yard together, providing more interaction and giving Amy plenty of response time to encourage easy conversation flow. Shirley has created a segment of private

"Amy time" each evening. Fred assures Amy that he loves her and takes her out for breakfast once a month and then to visit the pet store. The whole family profits from the unity these rituals bring, but especially Amy who feels a sense of uniqueness and security as a result of them.

In order to relate to Amy, both parents have been willing to disregard their natural tendencies, a principle Oldham and Morris suggest: "Successful parenting requires the ability to sacrifice for one's children and to expect little for oneself in return—to a point."[13] Amy doesn't need professional counseling, just respect and understanding. She has changed her opinion of her home, her parents, and her brother. Her overall attitude toward self-acceptance has matured.

The Meadows (INFP/ESTP/INFJ/ESTJ)

Mike (INFP), age 16, has difficulty getting along with his 13-year-old brother John (ESTP). Mike's father, Bob (ESTJ), lectures Mike mercilessly about keeping his car washed, cleaned, and serviced. Mike envies John's close relationship with his dad, as they do car and house repairs together. He wishes his dad would ask him to help. Mike has a few close friends but spends most of his time listening to music and working on the computer. He dislikes physical contact and constantly has to resist John's roughhousing. Marlene (INFJ), their mother, yells at them for wrestling in the house.

Even though John is younger, as a sensing thinker, he shows a lack of respect for softhearted, introspective Mike who leads with his heart. John teases Mike about being too softhearted and always needing approval. Bob attempts to toughen Mike by criticizing his "doormat" posture, which in turn makes Mike apologetic for how he is. Mike recently lost his girlfriend, and this has depressed him a lot. John taunts Mike and calls him a wimp because he takes things so personally. Bob orders John to "knock it off" and lectures Mike to "put the experience behind you and go on." Marlene is very supportive of Mike and listens sympathetically to his woes.

Marlene gripes at both boys about their messy room and complains about their clutter throughout the house and their uncompleted chores. Her anger bothers Mike more than John.

Because Mike and his mom share introversion and heart logic, they stick together on many matters. They've learned that it takes two feelers to persuade a thinker. However, when John and his dad, both extroverted thinkers, are in agreement, Mike and Marlene are nearly out of luck.

John and Mike's sibling rivalry greatly distresses Marlene, a sensitive feeler. She wants peace and harmony and for her sons to love each other. But Bob, who relies on cause-and-effect decisions along with muscle strength, ignores her pleas by saying "Boys will be boys; let them fight it out." This produces tension between the parents.

Evaluation

Introversion/Extroversion. Bob and John were amazed to learn that introversion is normal and not inferior. They assumed when someone didn't speak up it was because they had nothing to say; they did not realize the person just needed time to respond. Bob and John were also surprised that noise was louder to Marlene and Mike than to themselves. Marlene and Mike gained new self-respect knowing that their quietness was not inferior, which in turn helped them to speak up sooner and with more confidence.

Sensing/Intuition. Bob realizes that Mike, by nature, is not mechanical and has difficulty doing hands-on projects. Rather than assuming Mike is lazy or inept, Bob will have to work at accepting the differences between his two boys. Bob naturally respects what he himself can do and supposes any male can do the same. He easily approves of John's hands-on abilities. Bob will have to be careful not to compare John's hands-on achievements with Mike's attempts. Bob will need to ask Mike's opinion more and praise Mike for his ideas rather than his physical achievements

Thinking/Feeling. Unwittingly, a mother protects a feeling son from a thinking father or siblings, which causes havoc in the family or with other authority figures. Overprotection also produces the "mama's boy" syndrome. Male thinkers usually assume that all men are right and rugged and all women are weak, weepy, and wrong.

Feelers can learn to speak up and be honest about what they do or do not like or agree or disagree with, but they have to learn to tolerate the uneasiness that comes from not receiving approval or from inconveniencing someone. Strong-willed men like Bob feel a bit wimpy when they soften their talk and ways, but they, too, have to learn to tolerate what feels strange in order to respect the feeling people in the home. When a family learns that males can be legitimately feeling, they can encourage the feelers to give an honest answer even if it makes waves.

Structure/Spontaneity. Marlene and Bob now understand that their sons' spontaneity is normal; that spontaneous people, especially intuitives like Mike, are often unaware of clutter.

When structured people discover that spontaneous people resist immediate deadlines, they learn to project a long deadline, which in turn creates for spontaneous children the time necessary to let pressure and crisis build up—the stimulation needed to begin. Criticizing disorganized children does not help them. Structured people need to appreciate the fact that they have been gifted with the need to finish and have closure.

Blending

John has promised to try to be quieter in the morning and keep his music down. Bob vowed to give Mike and Marlene more time for response. Marlene and Mike agreed that they couldn't hurry their minds, but would try to be more understanding toward Bob and John's tendency to rush, talk, and be noisy.

Bob has pledged to be more patient and to affirm Mike for his computer and reasoning abilities. John now respects Mike's talents more. With renewed confidence, Mike and Marlene blend their compatible intuition to avoid family relationship problems and to mend current ones. John and Bob have accepted the legitimacy and value of Marlene and Mike's ideas and perception skills.

Marlene slowly admitted that she tends to protect Mike. When Bob was finally convinced that Mike's soft heart was God-designed and not caused by his mother, he eased up on both of them. John has accepted the revelation that his older brother is naturally tenderhearted and has shown new respect for him. The family has incorporated the use of "I" statements to eliminate sarcasm, name calling, and criticism. Bob has stopped lecturing since the coaching method works better.

Marlene and Bob have extended deadlines for Mike and John. They do not constantly worry their sons about cleaning up their rooms. Likewise, they have slightly softened their rigid standards regarding Mike's car and finished chores. The boys intentionally are trying to keep the common living area straightened.

The Meadows now laugh at what they used to argue about, and also boast that their family has access to every temperament preference. The mutual respect level in the family has risen significantly.

The Spanglers (ISFJ/ISFJ/ENTP/INFJ/ENTJ)

Jim and Donna Spangler are both ISFJs. Their children are Pete, age 16 (ENTP); Pam, age 14 (INFJ); and Jason, age 13 (INTJ). The children are each stronger than either parent. Jim and Donna are sensitive heart-logic people, striving for peace and harmony and avoiding confrontation. But the boys with their head logic enjoy a good argument and overturn many decisions, making light of their parents' passive approach. Pam defends her parents, but her perfectionistic attitude—from intuition— intimidates them, and she's no match for her brothers' thinking abilities.

Using their possibility thinking, these intuitive teens talk circles around their parents and feel justified in questioning and resisting parental instruction. Jim and Donna feel helpless, threatened, and out of control when the kids gang up on them. Teens suffer from insecurity when they're able to overpower their parents.

Blending

One family session informed the kids that introversion is normal for some men and not inferior or inadequate, and that the sensing preference is necessary for balanced decisions. Without apology and with renewed and unified confidence, Donna and Jim began to insist on adequate processing time, which sensing people need before making a decision. By sticking together and saying, "We say yes; we say no; we need more facts; we need more time to think," they can now handle difficult situations. Jim and Donna learned to consult their intuitive children before making final decisions, which gave the children a sense of importance. Jim and Donna's confidence as parents soared as did the security of their teens.

The Longs (INTP/ESFJ/ESTJ)

Ed Long (INTP) is an adult trying to deal with his childhood and adjust to the expectations of his parents, Rev. Long (ESFJ) and Mrs. Long (ESTJ). To illustrate an interesting example of the dynamics of family blending where all the children have more in common with each other than with a particular child, we include a list of Ed's adult siblings: brother (ESFJ), brother (ESTJ), sister (ISFJ), sister (ENFJ).

Mrs. Long preferred head logic and pretty much ran the home. Rev. Long consistently acquiesced to his wife. Ed was the oldest child, but he was only accepted when he behaved like extroverted, sensing, structured people do—the common thread in the Long family. His parents wanted him to be more like his traditional siblings.

As a young child, Ed always pleased his religious parents. He never questioned their authority regarding house rules or their desires for him to be involved in church. As early as age 12, Ed prepared and delivered sermons. His parents endeavored to direct him to study religion in college, but he chose philosophy instead. This was the first time he had ever disappointed them.

Although his mother approved of her husband's career as a minister, she blamed him for the family's low income because he would never ask for raises, which produced much family dissension.

"The lack of money in our home caused my mother to influence me toward making money," Ed shared. "My family always thought I was arrogant. My desire to study would never make any money, Mom would preach. Out of insecurity and lack of information, they kept me from the possible menus of life."

Ed was so hungry for learning and so fascinated with ideas, he continued as a student until he earned a Ph.D. As an adult, Ed enjoyed teaching philosophy and was involved in church, but after a few years he became restless. He questioned his own

religious experience and began investigating other religious per-
suasions. His interests in the abstract reached the point that he
spent all his free time and summer vacations studying and
traveling. Like a dry sponge, Ed couldn't seem to get enough
exposure to higher learning. He resembled a novice exploring a
huge cave with exciting new passages. Consequently, for a time
Ed neglected his wife, child, extended family, and church.

Evaluation

Ed's early life was so controlled, narrow, and sterile, he didn't
realize how deprived he was of options of learning until he was
out of the home. Because INTPs (only 1% of Americans) have
an insatiable hunger for knowledge, their complex temperaments demand exposure to broad and expansive options. INTPs
need a vast menu because they need constant challenges from
new perspectives. Parents of INTPs need encouragement and
guidance in exposing the possibilities that might satisfy the
inquisitiveness and curiosity of these very unusual creations of
God.

Ed's parents thought they were doing the best thing to guide
him toward their preferred subject of study and expertise, but
instead they drove Ed away from home. Sibling rivalry was a
great pressure, challenge, and disappointment in the Long family. Sibling rivalry and alienation have continued among the
adult Long children.

Blending

Ed's appreciation for and forgiveness of his parents' rigidity and
lack of vision came when he realized that they were not
equipped to understand who he was as a young adult. Now that
Ed understands the dynamics of family blending, one by one he
has been able to mend relationships with his siblings.

The Andrews brothers (ESFJ/ENTJ)

The case of the Andrews family— Clyde (ESTJ), Jan (ENFJ), Eric (ESFJ), and Dan (ENTJ)—emphasizes how parents can deal with the tension created when the oldest child is feeling and the younger one thinking, when one child is intuitive and the other sensing. We include the parents' temperaments to illustrate that sometimes the entire family is extroverted and structured.

At the persuasive suggestion of 16-year-old Eric, Clyde and Jan bought a race car track for 11-year-old Dan. Since Dan is not as mechanical as Eric, he was quite happy to have Eric's assistance in setting it up. They worked together happily for hours assembling and painting the little cars, building bridges and tunnels, and arranging tracks at various elevations.

Jan and Clyde raised their eyebrows when Eric invested in additional tracks and cars. It was soon apparent to them that he was more than just a bystander helping his younger brother. He had an interest in the operation himself.

Together the brothers bought a repair kit with extra gears and wheels and tools so they wouldn't have the expense and inconvenience of going to the hobby shop. The parents were pleased with the brothers' cooperative efforts and good rapport. Sparks began to fly, however. "We heard Dan yell, 'It's my track, I can kick it if I want to,' " Jan said. "'You can't kick my cars on my part of the track, or I'm not going to fix your cars.' Eric retorted."

Evaluation

Introversion/Extroversion. Because both boys are extroverted, loud arguments ensue. Because extroverts aren't sure what they're thinking until they hear themselves talk, and because they often speak too hastily, parents have to exercise tolerance for wordy and hurtful exchanges.

Sensing/Intuition. The Andrews family is split. Clyde and Eric prefer hands-on sensing and dealing with symptoms. Jan and Dan prefer preventive methods. Clyde wanted to ban both boys from the race track, but Jan wanted the boys to learn to get along.

Thinking/Feeling. The feeling preference Jan and Eric share demands harmony and causes Eric hurt feelings because Dan doesn't appreciate his generous assistance. Jan, like all feeling mothers, tends to protect the feeling son, even if he's the oldest. Yet Jan feels obligated to protect her youngest son, who really needs no protection. As thinkers, Clyde and Dan expect approval without question of their decisions or solutions. Even though Dan is younger than Eric, he's tougher skinned and does not worry about maintaining harmony or being sensitive to the feelings of others.

Structure/Spontaneity. Since the entire family is structured, they all want closure—and the sooner, the better.

Blending

Jan and Clyde were very concerned that their two boys couldn't get along, but they knew a solution existed. First, they analyzed the temperament tendencies of each. Jan asked both boys to make a list—her structure showing—of their grievances, beginning each sentence with an "I" statement. They grumbled about the size of the task, but each tackled it, because they were both structured. Writing their grievances down was better for feeling Eric who gets more emotional if he talks or hears accusations from another. Then they met for a family conference where each boy had the opportunity to share his gripes fully without comment from the other.

Softhearted Eric felt his hands-on sensing services were undervalued and taken for granted by his logical, intuitive little brother. This hurt his feelings. He disliked Dan bringing the cars for repair and expounding coldly that the majority of the track was his. Dan's only complaint was that Eric called him "klutz" when he accidentally kicked the track. Name calling violated Dan's intuitive reputation and annoyed him.

Writing down their frustrations clarified their perspective, exposed the simplicity of the problem, and paved the way for negotiation and compromise. At the conference Eric promised not to call Dan "klutz" anymore. Dan agreed to say nothing more about who owned most of the track, to assist Eric in repairs, and to be more careful with the equipment. From then on, the boys had a new appreciation of each other's preferences.

Conclusion

Learning about and applying temperament/type is like learning a new language requiring time and practice. Respecting each family member's natural design guarantees more harmony and cooperation among siblings. Accepting each child's individuality heightens self-esteem, helping children to discover and accept who God designed them to be and do.

TIP #12

Inspire self-discipline and independence.

- How can I control my kids?
- Should I spank my kids?
- How can I stop bad behavior?
- How can I make my kids obey?
- What's the best way to discipline?
- How can I get my kids to cooperate?
- Is there a way to instill self-discipline?
- What's the best and safest mode of punishment?
- Is there an easy way to teach children to make choices and be independent?
- How can I teach my kids to be responsible for gathering their supplies and being on time?
- How can I get my kids to admit their verbal/physical mistakes and accept consequences?
- How can I teach my feeling child to stick with his decision even if no friends join him?
- How can I encourage my child to trust her individuality although she is different from her friends?

As parents, all of us are concerned about these kinds of issues. We can be temperament literate, cognizant of communication skills, and have worthy goals set for our children, yet drop the ball when coaching them to become self-disciplined, inner motivated, and independent. How can we help our children to accept responsibility for their own attitudes and actions while developing self-confidence and a healthy self-worth?

Because children naturally resist authority and want things "my way," we must begin leading them toward self-discipline and independence when they are very young. As we celebrate their individuality and use the most respectful methods of constructive communication, we consistently, firmly, kindly, and slowly coach them to embrace self-discipline—which, in turn, leads to independence. However, maintaining consistent and diplomatic approaches to handling infractions demands the utmost maturity, patience, and self-control on our part.

Discipline vs. Punishment

A father recalls his father's whippings with a belt, sometimes applied days after the infraction. He'd be calmly watching television when his dad would order him upstairs for the beating he owed him. That was not discipline; it was abusive punishment. Punishment focuses on what is done; discipline focuses on what one can become.

Discipline is the process by which our children learn to adopt our standards as their own, a gradual process that continues throughout childhood. Discipline in its truest form means encouraging children to develop their own self-control so that they can ultimately be independent and responsible adults with a strong, reliable conscience. It is educating them to know what is expected of them and to respect the rights and property of others. Limits set on children's behavior both protect them from personal injury and prevent them from becoming social outcasts. When respectfully administered, far from building up feelings of frustration or resentment in children, discipline increases their sense of security.

Some parents are afraid to be firm and impose any type of restraint for fear of harming the emotional development of their children or diminishing their popularity as parents. Children expect, respect, and respond to consistency, but will constantly test the guidelines and parameters we set to make sure they are still safe. Nothing is more frustrating or damaging to the emotional growth of children than to be completely undisciplined. It is just as erroneous for us to be afraid that discipline will cause a breach in our relationship with our children. Undisciplined children are frustrated because they're never sure how important they are.

Good discipline demands a unified front. Both parents or authority figures must agree on rules and how to enforce them. Passing the buck from one parent to another or discussing parental differences in the earshot of children produces insecurity in children. They need to hear, "*We* say yes," or "*We* say no," and should never know which parent was for or against. Our youngest child presented us with a back-handed compliment when he was 16 by saying, "I'll tell you what's wrong with you two; you stick together." When children are taught self-discipline, they know that they belong and are important.

Instead of teaching their children self-discipline, however, some parents resort to physical punishment to correct unacceptable behavior. No doubt, that's how they were treated. Or perhaps it's because, as one parent confessed, "I spank when I'm embarrassed, inconvenienced, or angry. I know I need to talk it out with my children and suspend privileges instead." Spanking children for improper behavior builds up their fear of parental threat or fear of spanking instead of gaining new information to influence their decision making.

Although physical punishment is the fastest way to control children, it is the least creative and productive method. Physical punishment such as hitting, hair pulling, pinching, belting, spanking, slapping, and beating are all forms of power parenting. When authority figures hit children, they are teaching that violence is right and will solve problems, that people who love you are allowed to hurt you, that power and control get you what you want.

Instead of using the hand, we should use the head and be part of the abusive parenting cycle-breakers. Our goal should be positive discipline methods. According to Alice Miller,

> There will surely be some change in parent's behavior when they learn that what they have previously practiced in good faith as "necessary disciplining" is in reality a history of humiliating, hurting, and mistreating the child. Further, with increasing public understanding of the relationship between criminality and the experiences of early childhood, it is no longer a secret known only to the experts that every crime contains a concealed story, which can then be deciphered.[14]

Positive Discipline

Sometimes children misbehave simply because they are not mature enough to follow the rules without adult help. But as early as kindergarten age, with our guidance, they can understand the reasons behind rules. As they grow older, their limitations can be broadened for a greater sense of responsibility.

Spankings, administered with much self-control, should be used only in special instances when young children have been warned or reminded several times. When they are not used to spankings, the least little tap will accomplish your purpose. As soon as children can understand what is being done and why, other disciplinary methods should replace all little taps. Before discussing these options, note these principles of positive discipline:

• Convey your expectation of obedience.
• Allow children to express their viewpoints.
• Don't be afraid to admit you're wrong.
• Allow children the luxury of mistakes.
• Show appreciation for appropriate behavior, efforts, and improvements.
• Correct children in such a gracious way as to allow them to retain their dignity.

Time-Out

Even though using a "time-out chair" protects children's self-esteem and helps them learn proper behavior while cooling off, this method won't work 15 times a day. When using the time-out method, use as many minutes as the child is old—for instance, 4 minutes for a 4-year-old.

Positive Statements

When correcting children, use positive statements such as "Sand is not for throwing," or "Balls are not to be rolled in this room." If the inappropriate behavior continues, give prompt correction so that they will unmistakably associate the correction with the misdeed. A sharp but firm "no" and a disapproving look should take care of minor misbehavior. If not, physically remove them from the area, or take away the ball. After a while, they will be able to prevent themselves from throwing sand or a ball.

Choices

Offer choices: "Either your cowboy boots or your old sneakers." Use "I" statements to allow children to know exactly how you feel. "I feel frustrated when your good shoes are all muddy. I want you to learn to take care of your shoes."

Incentives

Offer incentives. Note, rewards to change behavior are considered bribes; rewards offered in exchange for good behavior are incentives. For example, a bribe is: "Here's a piece of gum; now stop whispering." An incentive is: "We'll be sitting a long time, so if you can keep quiet while I'm in this meeting, we'll stop by the playground on the way home."

The point system works well with preschool and younger elementary children. They may receive 1 point for being on time, making their beds, brushing their teeth, or putting dishes in the dishwasher. A 5-point job may include volunteering to do an extra job or assisting a younger child. A 10-point job would be helping to rake the yard. Earned points may be redeemed for money to put in the bank or for a privilege or a movie ticket.

Chores

Assign chores in exchange for infractions. When older children and teens talk back, assign them a 5-minute chore they choose from a list. Upgrade the chore according to age. When they balk at following instructions, remove a privilege such as riding their bikes, watching a T.V. program, playing with the computer, using the phone, being with a friend, or using the car. Ask their opinions on privilege removal.

Once when our oldest son broke the rules, we consulted him about how he should be disciplined. "Take my bike for 2 weeks?" he conjectured. He was aware of what suspension would make the most impression. "How about 2 days?" we bargained.

Discussions

Always discuss your children's inappropriate behavior with them. When an offense occurs in public, make an appointment to talk to your children later. Even at home, give them a few minutes to think about what you and they are going to discuss. This put-off allows you time to cool off and avoids impulsive, rash decisions.

Discussions of any kind take time, thought, and patience, but if you will regard time as an investment made in your children's emotional maturity account, the dividends will be forthcoming for you and your child and extending even to your grandchildren.

*****

The methods of positive discipline are numerous, but the ultimate goal is the same: to inspire children to become self-controlled and independent young people, properly prepared for leaving the home and living productive lives. If our children are reared with positive parenting methods, they will, in turn, become positive adults and, ultimately, positive parents themselves.

Encouraging Independence

Leaving home should be a time of celebration. Our counseling experiences reveal, however, that many exits from home are unpleasant or not happening at all. Our goal then, as parents, is to prepare older teens to understand who they are and to respect and accept themselves enough to leave the nest to attend college, work, and/or marry.

The process of "letting go" actually starts in the first years of life, but becoming separate in a psychological sense is a lifelong process—continually building on, reaffirming, and refining a sense of self. The trek into adulthood goes through virgin territory. We parents can erect caution lights here and there, warn of pitfalls, build up anticipation for the joy and rigors of the trip, and provide sketchy maps with alternative routes. But that is about all we can do besides pray. Falling or tripping does not signal failure, but gives young people the opportunity to check the reason for the fall and analyze their reactions.

We must release our children at a gradual pace and in certain areas until they grab the reins themselves. Momentum may slow, and there may even be a "jerk" in the takeover as they decide on their comfortable speed of gait and find the terrain they prefer. Teens will test their ability with new experiences. They may seem mature, but reactions to changes will reveal their need for continued guidance.

This need for guidance turns toward a desire for support. Teens and young adults need to know where we stand on moral issues. We graduate from our role as mentors and become consultants. As our children become independent single or married adults, alterations will occur in family relationships, with each new situation demanding understanding and acceptance. We should be careful to offer advice to adult children *only* when asked and then give it sparingly.

Conclusion

The blending of family temperament preferences infused with diplomatic dialogue is the healthiest and most pleasant way to lead children to accept and love themselves and others. Adopting good attitudes and values helps them live creatively and productively and be confident enough to leave home at the appropriate time on their way to a lifetime of fulfillment. We want you to be good friends with your children and to observe them passing on positive parenting techniques to their children.

We trust that you will enjoy your high calling as a parent. You'll always be a parent, no matter how old your child is. Remember that each child, young or grown, is like a flower bulb waiting to blossom. Believe us, grandparenting is worth all the struggles of being parents.

Oh, God, Make Me a Better Parent

Help me to understand my children, to listen patiently to what they have to say, and to answer all their questions kindly. Keep me from interrupting them, talking back to them, and contradicting them. Make me as courteous to them as I would have them be to me. Give me the courage to confess my sins against my children and to ask of them forgiveness, when I know that I have done them wrong.

May I not vainly hurt the feelings of my children. Forbid that I should laugh at their mistakes or resort to shame and ridicule as punishment. Let me not tempt a child to lie and steal. So guide me hour by hour that I may demonstrate by all I say and do that honesty produces happiness.

Reduce, I pray, the meanness in me. May I cease to nag; and when I am out of sorts, help me, Oh Lord, to hold my tongue.

Blind me to the little errors of my children, and help me to see the good things they do. Give me a ready word for honest praise.

Help me to treat my children as those of their own age, but let me not exact of them the judgments and conventions of adults. Allow me not to rob them of the opportunity to wait upon themselves, to think, to choose, and to make decisions.

Forbid that I should ever punish them for my selfish satisfaction. May I grant them all of their wishes that are reasonable and have the courage always to withhold a privilege I know will do them harm.

Make me so fair and just, so considerate and companionable to my children that they will have a genuine esteem for me. Fit me to be loved and imitated by my children.

With all thy gifts, Oh God, do give me calm and poise and self-control.[15]

—Garry C. Myers

Notes

[1] Scott Peck, *A World Waiting to Be Born* (New York: Bantam Books/Doubleday/Dell, 1993) 163.

[2] Haim Ginott, *Between Parent and Child* (New York: Avon Books/Macmillan, 1965) 67-68.

[3] Alice Miller, *For Your Own Good* (New York: Farrar, Straus, & Giroux, 1983) 98.

[4] John M. Oldham and Lois B. Morris, *Personality Self-Portrait* (New York: Bantam Books, 1990) 368.

[5] Ruth Ward, *Blending Temperament—Improving Relationships* (Grand Rapids: Baker Book House, 1988) 25.

[6] Ibid., 26.

[7] Ruth Ward, *Self Esteem—Gift from God* Grand Rapids: Baker Book House, 1989) 97.

[8] Ward, *Blending Temperaments,* 28.

[9] Ward, *Self Esteem,* 128.

[10] Ibid., 131.

[11] Ibid., 141.

[12] Miller, 98.

[13] Oldham and Morris, 313.

[14] Miller, 206.

[15] Garry C. Myers, *Highlights.* Used by permission of Highlights for Children, Inc., Columbus OH. Copyrighted material.

Suggested Readings

Clayton, Lynn. *10 Gifts Your Children Will Grow to Appreciate.* Macon GA: Smyth & Helwys, 1998.

Cloud, Henry, and John Townsend. *Boundaries with Kids.* Grand Rapids: Zondervan, 1998.

Coburn, Karen Levin, and Madge Lawrence Tregger. *Letting Go—A Parents' Guide to Today's College Experience.* Bethesda MD: Adler & Adler, 1992.

Miller, Alice. *For Your Own Good: Hidden Cruelty in Child Rearing and the Roots of Violence.* New York: Farrar, Straus, Giroux, 1990.

Oldham, John M., and Lois B. Morris. *The Personality Self-Portrait.* New York: Bantam Books, 1990.

Peck, M. Scott. *The Road Less Traveled.* New York: Simon & Schuster, 1978.

_____. *A World Waiting to Be Born.* New York: Bantam Books, 1993.

_____. *People of the Lie.* New York: Simon & Schuster, 1983.

Rainey, Dennis, with David Boehi. *The Tribute and the Promise.* Nashville: Thomas Nelson, 1994.

Tournier, Paul. *The Strong and the Weak.* Philadelphia PA: Westminster Press, 1963.

_____. *A Place for You.* New York: Harper and Row, 1968.

_____. *To Understand Each Other.* Louisville KY: John Knox Press, 1970.